In the book of Revelation we're told that we will overcome by the blood of the Lamb and the word of our testimony. From that passage, we can understand that the testimony God gives us is important and life changing. What a shame if we were to lose or forget it! Praise God that Ron has written down in *You Want Me to Do What!?!* a series of powerful stories that are sure to encourage you and bolster your faith in our Mighty God. We in the worldwide ministry of Evangelism Explosion are grateful to God for Ron's calling and service in building the work in Africa!

— DR. JOHN B. SORENSEN, D.D., D.H.L.
PRESIDENT / CEO EVANGELISM EXPLOSION
INTERNATIONAL, WWW.EVANGELISMEXPLOSION.ORG

Ron Tyler is a leader of leaders. He has trained thousands of people around the globe to share their faith in Christ. Many more thousands have come to a saving faith in Jesus Christ through Ron Tyler's ministry. Ron has experienced some of the most incredible God moments. Through his years of faith and obedience, God has shown up in extraordinary ways. *You Want Me to Do What!?!* is a must read. I promise it will encourage you and impact your faith journey in a profound way!

— DR. JODY G. RAY, LEAD PASTOR, MT BETHEL
CHURCH, WWW.MTBETHEL.ORG

Ron's obedience to the call of our Heavenly Father placed him in a position to achieve astounding results for the Evangelism Explosion ministry in Africa. The success was punctuated by numerous miraculous interventions and orchestrated by the Holy Spirit, leading to the greatest miracle of all—the salvation of millions of precious souls across the African continent.

My prayer is that the Holy Spirit will ignite a flame within the heart of every person who reads this book, giving them a burning desire and commitment to make *their* lives count for the Kingdom of God.

— MALCOLM THOMAS, CHAIRMAN, EVANGELISM
EXPLOSION SOUTH AFRICA

Dr. Ron Tyler and I served together in the ministry of Evangelism Explosion for almost 30 years. As the Executive Pastor at Houston's First Baptist Church, I organized support for Ron's vital work in Africa. Later as a member EE's International Board of Directors, I was thrilled to hear quarterly detailed reports of the growth and success of his pioneering work in the 53 nations of this continent.

I am thrilled that he has documented God's miraculous work, sharing his encouraging testimonies of answered prayer, transformed lives, and the spectacular spread of the gospel throughout a continent. I highly endorse his book, *You Want Me to Do What!?!*

— DAVID SELF, BOARD CHAIR, EVANGELISM
EXPLOSION INTERNATIONAL

This book recounts Dr. Ron Tyler's astonishing real-life experiences of encounters with Jesus. It contains gripping tales of how one missionary helps millions all over Africa come to saving faith in Christ. I highly recommend!

— JAMES C. BROOKS, FORMER CEO IN THE USA
OPERATIONS OF ING

I first met Ron Tyler in the late 1990s when he was the VP of Evangelism Explosion, responsible for spreading the Gospel to the entire continent of Africa. I still remember thinking, *Africa is a big place, how does one man do all of that?* Matthew 19:26, "With men this is impossible, but with God all things are possible."

After some of Ron's extensive trips abroad, evangelizing, teaching, and spreading the Good News of Jesus, we would visit and I would listen to his amazing stories. But this book is more than just Ron's stories—it's a picture of how God, even today, can use a single obedient man to bring about his promises, leading to the salvation of countless people.

— TERRY FRIERSON, RETIRED BUSINESSMAN

YOU WANT ME TO DO WHAT!?!

HOW GOD SAVED 25 MILLION PEOPLE THROUGH ONE MISSIONARY FAMILY'S OBEDIENCE

RON TYLER

Foreword by
KAY ARTHUR

CALLED WRITERS
CHRISTIAN PUBLISHING

DEDICATION

+*For the hundreds of thousands of Christians trained who continue to share the Gospel to millions and millions of people—people who will now live in Heaven for eternity.*

+*For Timothy and Ann Marie, our children who traveled to Africa and left their life in the USA as their parents followed the Lord's Vision.*

+*For Belinda, my loving wife who was obedient to the Lord and willing to support me in moving from the comforts of the corporate world to the pastorate in the USA, and then to the ends of the earth, I will always cherish. As engraved on the inside of both of our wedding rings the initials: "MTYLTT" - I will love you, More Than Yesterday Less Than Tomorrow.*

+*For Rick Posey and all who have prayed, listened, encouraged, and walked along side me through the book development.*

+*For Kay Arthur who taught me to love the Scriptures, to believe that I can trust Jesus in all situations, to walk daily with Him every step of the way, and to know that with God nothing will be impossible.*

I, Ron Tyler, a husband, a father, a friend, and a Christian, who joyously walks with Jesus, A Way of Life, that goes On and On...

I am grateful and thankful for Bob Singleton, a retired SVP and CFO of the 2nd largest USA newspaper publisher, a lifelong musician, a jazz trumpet player, who composed numerous pieces of music, and a former EE International Board member, after hearing me present my annual reports, wrote and dedicated two songs to me. The titles and words are:

A Way of Life!

A Way of Life, For all to see,
A Way of Life, For you and me,
A Way of Life, For everyone,
who trust in Jesus, God's only Son!
A Way of Life Because of Him,
who paid the price for all my sin,
A Way of Life, A Gift that's free,
A Way of Life for All Eternity!

On and On!

The light shines brightest in the darkness,
So let it shine for all to see.
For the grace of God is there for His chosen,

And I know that He has chosen me.
So I joyfully tell the story,
How He reached down and made me whole.
On that day He touched me and set me free,
He put His light inside my soul.
On and On, we go on and on!
'Til the last soul has heard the Good News;
That Jesus Christ will forgive the sin of all,
who place their trust in Him.

A Scripture that encourages all to live out the Gospel as "A Way of Life" that goes "On and On" to every generation is Psalm 145:3-4,5b-6. May it be a theme for your life, as it is for Belinda and me.

"Great is the LORD, and highly to be praised,
And His greatness is unsearchable.
One generation shall praise Your works to another,
And shall declare Your mighty acts . . .
And on Your wonderful works, I will meditate.
Men shall speak of the power of Your awesome acts,
And I will tell of Your greatness."

CONTENTS

COPYRIGHT

Published by Called Writers Christian Publishing, LLC

Tuscaloosa, Alabama

Print version ISBN: 978-1-7354760-8-7

FOREWORD

KAY ARTHUR

You Want Me to do **WHAT!?!**

Hang on, Beloved of God, for eye has not seen, ear has not heard what God has prepared for those who love Him. We are living epistles to be read and known of all men, putty in the hands of the Divine Potter.

Do you know what manner of love God has bestowed upon you, that you, my brother or sister, should be called a child of God? We live not by might, nor by power, but by His indwelling Spirit and He promises that He will never leave us nor forsake us, so that we might be called the children of God.

Scripture, God's life-giving, breathed word tells us that we don't know what we will be like, but we know that when we see Him, we will be like Him.

Knowing this should cause us to purify ourselves as He is pure and live by His every word! And what do you think that might look like? I think it might look like what this book, *You Want Me To Do What!?!*, is all about!

Ron and Belinda Tyler and I have a long history through Precept, which you will learn more about as you read his book, yet we have not been in touch for several decades.

I am 89 years old and feel so blessed to be asked to write the Foreword to what Ron has shared with us. In fact, I believe His book and the invitation to read it is a sweet gift from our Lord.

Ron's book is an absolute delight! It's rich in example after example of living by faith, by every word that comes from the mouth of God. It's about trusting Him—a living testimony of what it is to know God, to believe His Word, and to live by His precepts. Practical. A faith builder. Challenging. Captivating.

Take a good look at the "Table of Contents," start reading, and see for yourself how relevant, rich, practical, exciting, and down to earth it is—but watch out! I didn't want to put it down.

I wanted to keep on reading and learning, so I could do what He, my God, my Father, my Savior and Lord wants, and consequently hear His "well done, my good and faithful servant."

As you read Ron's book, you will see it was written out of obedience to the Spirit of God. This book caused me to stop and reflect on my own life. I asked myself, "What are people seeing and learning about God through the way I navigate life, Parkinson's?" I have been so blessed and I believe you, too, will be blessed, encouraged, inspired, and drawn even closer to the Lord.

— KAY ARTHUR, BESTSELLING AUTHOR AND
BRAND AMBASSADOR OF PRECEPT,
WWW.PRECEPT.ORG

INTRODUCTION

I had just finished visiting the nation of Central African Republic. In Bangui, the capital city, I boarded an airplane to return home to Nairobi.

On the first leg of the flight home, we landed in Brazzaville, Congo, for a layover. It was late at night, about two o'clock in the morning. All the passengers got off the airplane and were escorted to a separate building next to the airport, which was closed. All passengers, including myself, gave our tickets and passports to the attendant sitting at a desk.

We sat for about two hours before he began to call the name of each passenger who had departed the last plane. The attendant gave each passenger his or her ticket and passport back. Then the passenger was to walk outside and board the next flight.

While waiting, I discovered I was not to get on this particular airplane, but on another one that would leave later that morning. Every passenger in the room received their ticket and passport and left.

Being the only one in the room, the attendant looked at me as if I were a bit of a nuisance. He motioned for me to come to him. He gave me my ticket and passport while saying something to me in French. My confusion must have been evident because he stopped talking and began motioning what he wanted me to do.

He pointed toward another door, which led outside to the airport parking lot. Moving his hand, I interpreted that I was supposed to go through that door. He turned his hand, symbolizing that he planned to lock it behind me.

"I understand," I said. "Leave this room and go outside!"

I took my luggage and walked outside into the dark of night. The moon was shining, so there was a small amount of light. But not much.

Next to the building was the airport entrance. It, too, was locked for the night, though airport personnel milled around inside. The attendant left the separate building where I had been waiting. I assumed he went home.

I looked around and saw a bench, walked over to it with my luggage, and sat down. I thought, *This is crazy! And dangerous! I am out in the dark, with no security, all by myself.*

But what else could I do? Nothing but sit and wait until the airport reopened so that I could board my flight to Nairobi, Kenya.

I sat, thinking, praying, and waiting for the time to pass. As I prayed, I remembered that I was not alone—that Jesus had promised, "I will never leave you, nor forsake you." I clung tightly to these words of assurance, reminding myself of them over and over.

Around 5:30 in the morning, I looked at my watch and noticed there was no sunrise peaking over the horizon at all. It was still completely dark out. There were no lights in the parking lot. The bench was not very comfortable, but it was better than sitting on the ground.

All was quiet. For a moment.

Suddenly, I heard the ear-piercing sound of gunfire. I saw a flash of light to my right. It was only about 30 feet away! Then I heard another round of gunfire to my left, followed by more flashes of light.

I prayed, "Lord, where should I run?" I kept thinking, *I should get under the bench.* I listened and heard the answer, "Run into the arms of Jesus—Do not move!"

Things can happen very quickly in life. In the blink of an eye or the flash of a pistol, everything can change. You can be working in a corporate office in Atlanta one day, and then a very short time later, be a missionary sitting on a bench in Africa between two men who are exchanging gunfire.

What follows is my story—fifty stories, to be exact, that I want to share with you. They're the stories of a man who believed God to accomplish the impossible. They're the stories of a family who trusted God deeply, uprooting every aspect of their lives and moving to another continent to answer His call.

But most of all, these are the stories of Jesus—the stories of His power unleashed through prayer, rejoicing, and even sorrow.

I pray that as you read these stories, God reveals to you both His faithfulness and His love. I pray that your trust in God grows exponentially. I pray that if you don't already, you will begin to believe His Word and His promises to you. I pray that you are encouraged to answer His call—to whatever place and position that may be.

Because where God calls you, He is already there, waiting to welcome you as you run into the arms of Jesus.

1

MORE THAN A SUNDAY AFFAIR

In early 1973, I was sitting by myself at the hotel bar after a 10-hour workday. I was a young professional working for Southern Services, a company that would now be classified as an IT company. I was thinking, *I have a beautiful wife. A great job. We just got through designing our dream home, and the contractor has already started on it. These are exciting times!*

So why do I feel so empty?

I have everything, as far as I can see. I'm only 24 years old! But something is missing. There must be more to life than this . . .

Returning to my hotel room, I walked over to the bed and unzipped my suitcase. A very small, thin book was inside. I was not in the habit of reading books for leisure, but this night was different.

My mother had given me this book, but I really had no plans to read it. Even when I had thrown it in my suitcase, I only thought, *Maybe I'll get around to reading this one day . . .*

But when I picked up the book, I figured tonight was the

night. The book was *Prison to Praise* by Merlin Carothers. *Strange title*, I thought, before promptly devouring the entire book. In it, a man who had been an army officer and pastor told strange tales of the supernatural workings of Jesus Christ. But not tales from Bible times. No, this man gave accounts indicating that Jesus is still alive and working powerfully on the earth today!

The next morning I began the three-hour drive back to Atlanta from Birmingham. As I drove down the long straightaways of I-20, one specific thought kept coming back to my mind: *Christianity is much more than just a Sunday affair. It's much more than just going to church on Sunday.*

This was a new concept for me. My parents had taken my brother and me to church every Sunday growing up. I had gone through confirmation classes and joined the church. As a teenager, I had been active in the youth department, which basically meant that I came to most of the youth events.

Being from the South, especially during those years, everyone went to church. It was just what you did. Everyone considered it "the right thing to do." Plus, you could add the name of your church and the positions you held to your resume.

As I reflected on this, I began to wonder why I didn't have the answer even with all of that background in church. Why didn't I know why I felt so empty? Driving past the Six Flags Over Georgia amusement park, I prayed a one-sentence prayer that would change my life forever.

"God, if You are real, then come into my life."

Right at that exact moment, something happened. All-of-a-sudden, I had this realization that Jesus is real! He is the Truth!

I realized that I was not alone, and from that moment in my life, at 24 years old, I have never been alone again. Jesus Christ became my Lord and my Savior, changing everything about me and my future.

What about you—do you feel alone? Do you feel like something is missing from your life?

If that is you, I can tell you with complete confidence that there is much more to life than what you're currently experiencing.

Jesus Christ is patiently waiting for you to invite Him into your life. He is knocking at the door of your heart and saying, "Are you ready to welcome Me in today?"

2

BUT I KNOW NOTHING ABOUT CARS!

By December of 1973, I had been a Christian for maybe six months. My wife Belinda and I decided to drive over to Madison, Georgia, on Christmas Eve to celebrate Christmas with her family.

While on the way, our car went dead without warning. I pulled over on the shoulder and rolled to a stop. It was late in the afternoon, so there were very few cars on the interstate at the time. As a new Christian, I had been taught to thank God in all things, and for all things. This seemed like the perfect opportunity to put that teaching into practice.

So I prayed, "Thank You, Lord, that our car has stopped working. I don't know why this has happened, but I trust You know why!"

Next, I got out of the car and opened the hood. I knew very little about cars. Honestly, I'm not sure what I was expecting to see. Amazingly, another car pulled up behind ours right at that moment.

A man got out and said, "Hi, there! Are you having some car trouble?"

"Yes, it just stopped working and I'm not sure why."

The man looked under the hood for just a few seconds, then said, "Come with me!"

The man seemed trustworthy and confident, so I asked Belinda if she would mind staying in the car for a few minutes while I rode with this man to get help.

Back in those days, most gas stations had a mechanic and some basic car parts stocked. We drove to one such gas station and the man got out, talked to the mechanic for a minute, then came back with a rubber belt for my car.

When we got back, the man grabbed a toolbox from his trunk and promptly went to work installing the new belt. Once he finished, he told me to start the car. I did, and everything was working perfectly!

Before getting back on the interstate, I prayed again. "Thank You, Lord, for sending that man to fix our car." Then we drove on over to Madison for a nice Christmas celebration.

You may be in a situation that you don't understand right now. Maybe it seems inconvenient, frustrating, or even unfair. During those times, our temptation is often to fall into self-pity, complaining, or grumbling. But the Bible says, "In everything give thanks, for this is the will of God for you in Christ Jesus" (1 Thessalonians 5:18, NASB).

If you don't know where to turn or what to do, start by thanking God for the situation!

3

PLEASE SEND RAIN, LORD

My mother called and asked if Belinda and I would go to a Christian retreat for the weekend. The retreat started on Friday evening and ran through Sunday afternoon. My initial response was noncommittal, so my mother threw in a few extra details that she hoped would sweeten the deal.

"The retreat center has a tennis court, and the motel where we're staying has a swimming pool."

I told my mother, "Okay, we'll go, but only if it rains on Friday. I have a softball game on Friday, and I have a responsibility to the team to be there. But if the game gets rained out, we can go to the retreat."

It was June of 1975, and I was working as a programmer analyst in downtown Atlanta. My office was located in the First National Bank building, which, at 44 stories, was the tallest building in Atlanta at the time.[1] I had a beautiful view with floor-to-ceiling glass windows all around.

When Friday rolled around, I sat staring out those windows, noticing sadly that there was not a single cloud in the sky. I had begun to really want to go to the retreat, but it was not looking good. As the day wore on, my hope was wearing thin. There would be no blessing that day to come via rain clouds.

Or so I thought.

About 3 pm, a very large, dark cloud began moving rapidly across the city sky, before stopping right over the top of downtown Atlanta. A heavy downpour ensued for about 30 minutes straight.

Back then, the city had a sports department you could call to find out if games were canceled due to weather. So around 4 pm, I called the number and sure enough, all games were canceled due to rain. Immediately, I let my mother know we would be going on the retreat.

That retreat ended up having a profound impact on our lives and on our callings in the Lord. In fact, Belinda received Christ as her Savior at this retreat! Like me, she had grown up in church, but she did not have a personal relationship with the Lord. She had never truly known the Lord until that weekend.

And it all happened because of a very short, powerful storm that popped up in Atlanta out of nowhere. Years later, I found out what my mother had been up to that Friday.

Early that morning, she had gotten up and prayed earnestly, "Lord, please send rain!" She had no way of knowing how influential this retreat would be on us, but she did have a strong desire for us to attend. So she prayed for

God to send rain, and sure enough, He answered—in quite a dramatic fashion.

Not only did He send a large downpour of rain that seemed to appear out of nowhere, but He put His signature on it! The thunderstorm had been so strong at my parents' house, that lightning had struck a tree in their yard, leaving a long, black burn streak right down the middle of the tree. The insurance company sent an inspector out who determined that the tree would inevitably die. So their insurance company offered to pay to have the tree removed.

But my parents decided to leave the tree as a memorial for what God had done that day. It never died, and in fact, it's still there today, reminding us of God's love and faithfulness.

You see, God wasn't just answering my mother's prayer for rain that day. He was also in the process of answering the prayers of everyone who had prayed for Belinda's salvation, for God's plans and purposes in our lives to prevail, and other such prayers.

Whatever you're praying and believing for, you can rest in the truth that God is faithful. Keep praying and believing until you see the answer. But do it from a place of trust.

"Let's hold firmly to the confession of our hope without wavering, for He who promised is faithful" (Hebrews 10:23, NASB).

4

IS THERE ANYTHING IN MY LIFE THAT I NEED TO CLEAN UP?

In August of 1975, Belinda and I were in the process of selling our house. We had it listed for sale by owner, and had run an ad in the Atlanta Journal-Constitution, which was a very effective method for getting the word out about pretty much anything in those days.

Several people called to inquire about the house, and one person seemed very interested. He wanted our address, but he did not want to make an appointment to see the house, which I thought was a little odd. Still, I gave him the address and hoped I would hear back from him later.

It was only a few days before I received a letter from this man in the mail. However, he wasn't interested at all in buying our house. He was only interested to sell me an informational packet about how to sell a house. His business was to sell these informational packets that also included a "For Sale" sign you could put in your front yard.

For some reason, I was extremely bothered by this man.

I felt that he had used deception to obtain my information, and that offended me. When I got that packet, I was ready to give him a piece of my mind.

So that's exactly what I did. I called him—perhaps ironically, with no intention of purchasing what he was selling—to let him know what I thought about his business practices.

"Do you sell a packet that helps homeowners sell their houses?" I asked.

I could hear the excitement in the man's voice when he responded, "Why, yes! Yes, I do!"

Immediately I began letting him know that I did not appreciate the way he disguised himself as a prospective buyer in order to obtain my address. I told him that it was deceptive, and that he should have simply told me the real reason why he was calling me.

Our conversation ended abruptly. I really thought I was going to feel better after letting this man know what I thought. Instead, I felt very strange about the whole thing. In fact, I did not feel any better at all. Now I felt worse!

That just wasn't the way I usually talked to people. Yes, the salesman had been wrong for what he did. But now I felt that my response was wrong as well.

Still, I resisted any attempt at correcting my behavior. Instead, I took his letter, placed it back in the envelope, and put it in the kitchen trash. However, it obviously continued to weigh on me because later in the day, out of fear that God might try to get me to call the man back, I took the kitchen trash and put it into the outside garbage can. I couldn't get rid of that letter quickly enough.

I felt a sense of relief when the garbage was picked up the next morning.

However, the relief didn't last. A few days later, during my prayer time, I felt led to ask God, "Lord, is there anything in my life that I need to clean up?"

I waited quietly. Hoping for a "No." Wanting to just move on . . . But then came the still, small voice.

"Yes. Do you remember the man you called about his home selling packet?"

Immediately I thought, *Oh no!* But then quick relief came when I remembered, *Ah, yes . . . but the letter is gone! I'm safe!*

In my mind, I just said back to the Lord, "Yes, Lord, I know that was wrong. I should not have called that man and said those unkind words to him. I knew you would want me to call him back and apologize . . ." I conceded, before continuing, ". . . and you know, I would call him back, but I put the letter in the garbage, and the garbage has already been picked up. And I don't remember the salesman's name or telephone number. I don't know how to get in touch with him."

At that point, God prompted me to go get the Atlanta phone book. I went and grabbed it and then sat there silently, waiting. I thought, *I don't want to know the man's number. I don't want to remember his name!*

But I kept quiet and waited, and after a while, God brought the man's last name to my memory.

I opened up the phone book and found the section with his last name. There were about 14 people with the same last name, so I thought, *Well, I guess I will call every single one of them until I find this salesman.*

Before I even started, I felt the Lord prompt me, "Just look down the page."

As my eyes began to scroll down the page, all-of-a-sudden, I remembered the man's first name. Finding it in the list, I promptly gave him a call.

"Hi, I am in the process of selling my house. Do you have a company that offers a sales packet for homeowners looking to sell their house?"

Again, I could hear the excitement in the man's voice. "Yes, I do!" he answered, before starting his sales pitch.

I thought, *Yep, this is the right person,* before taking a deep breath. I felt like a spear went right through my heart.

What am I doing? I thought, before biting the bullet and launching into my apology.

"Several days ago, I received your letter and called you. I did not appreciate the way you disguised yourself as a prospective buyer, and I let you know that over the phone. But I am a Christian, and I should not have said those things to you. I was wrong, and I'm sorry."

The man accepted my apology.

Then he asked, "Are you sure you don't want to buy one of my packets?"

I still had no interest in the packet, of course, so I politely responded, "No, thank you," before getting off of the phone with him.

Immediately afterward, I felt a release and a sense of true peace. I had prayed, listened to God, and then obeyed.

I was now able to move forward free and clear.

What about you? Are you willing to be bold and ask God that same question: Is there anything in my life I need to clean up?

For some reason, we dread asking that question, as though God is going to make us do something awful or embarrassing. But that's not how He operates. His goal isn't to have us do something awkward or uncomfortable. His goal is to get us to a place of peace and freedom.

Let Him take you to that place today, friend! You won't regret it!

5

GIVE ME THE GREAT FAITH OF THESE MEN

When my mother prayed for rain that day in June of 1975, it affected Belinda's eternity, but it also had a lasting impact on our lives. No one could have known it at the time, but that Christian retreat was simply the beginning of a series of events that would impact numerous lives and eternities!

The Christian retreat turned out to be run by a couple named Jack and Kay Arthur. At that time, theirs was a relatively new ministry called "Reach Out", which essentially consisted of a 32-acre farm in Chattanooga, Tennessee, where teens and adults would come to learn teachings on how to study the Bible more effectively.

Reach Out would later be renamed Precept Ministries International. It is a large, very active ministry to this day, impacting hundreds of millions of people in more than 180 countries. Of course, both Jack and Kay would go on to become well-known figures in the world of Christian ministry. But Kay especially would become quite "famous" as a bestselling author of more than 100 books and Bible studies, as well as hosting her own radio and television shows.

At this weekend retreat, Kay talked about an upcoming week-long retreat called "Boot Camp." Boot Camp was designed for youth, but anyone could come and learn. It was to be held the very next month, in July of 1975.

Belinda kept feeling that we should go to Boot Camp, but it happened to be on the exact same dates we were scheduled for a vacation. We had already booked a condo on the beach in Destin, Florida, and Belinda absolutely loves the beach! She wrestled with whether or not she should even mention Boot Camp to me. She was afraid of missing out on our beach vacation.

However, it turned out that we were able to simply reschedule our beach trip for the next week after Boot Camp, so God worked it out for us to do both!

As I mentioned, most of the attendees at Boot Camp were teenagers, as it was designed to be a youth retreat. However, several adults were in attendance, including Belinda and me.

During the event, Kay asked the adults to join her in praying for the teenagers who were there. There were only a few of us, and we each took turns praying out loud. While praying for the teenagers, I felt this prompting rise up in me to pray, out loud in front of everyone, "Lord, I will be anything you want me to be! I will go anywhere you want me to go! I will do anything you want me to do!"

Right at that moment, I heard in my spirit a very clear

response from the Lord: "I am going to use you to reach hundreds of thousands of people for Me."

Of course, no one else heard it. But I knew for sure what I had heard!

Belinda and I went back to our room that evening, and I shared with her what I believed God had very clearly said to me.

Now, keep in mind, we had only been Christians for a very short time. I had asked Jesus to be my Savior about 22 months prior, and Belinda only about 1 month prior. Neither of us had any idea or intention to ever go into ministry.

So this revelation was quite strange and dramatic to both of us.

Still, I was absolutely certain. I was so certain, in fact, that I told Belinda, "When we get home, I'm going to apply for seminary, quit my job, and sell our house!"

Later at Boot Camp, Belinda and I were praying and strongly considering everything we were experiencing. We thought it would be a good idea to invite Jack and Kay to come with us on our beach vacation, and they gladly agreed. They also decided to bring their son, David, and two of their staff members, Rick, a male staff member, and JoAnn, a female staff member.

Jack pulled their camper and the men of his group stayed in it. Kay and JoAnn stayed with Belinda and me in the condo. Kay had recommended several books to me, and my plan was to at least start reading them during our vacation.

The books were all about men of great faith who had

seen God accomplish the impossible in their lives. Excitedly, I devoured three of these books in that single week. One was about Hudson Taylor, a British missionary who undertook radical measures to spread the gospel in China in the 1800s. He founded a missionary organization under the premise that they would never ask any human being for money, but would rely directly on God to provide for their needs. The organization prospered and remains in operation to this day.

George Mueller was another. He is known for founding and operating Christian orphanages throughout England. Just like Taylor, Mueller vowed to never once ask any human being for money to support the work, and sure enough, God showed up time after time, with millions of dollars passing through Mueller's hands over the years.

C.T. Studd was the last man I read about. He was the son of a wealthy agricultural tycoon, which meant he had a very large inheritance. Studd was also a famous athlete—considered the top cricket player in England in his playing days. But at a very young age, he gave up his easy life, gave away all of his financial wealth, and became a missionary to China, and then later, to India and Africa. He explained his decision by saying, "How could I spend the best years of my life living for the honors of this world when thousands of souls are perishing every day?"

Studd also wrote, in his poem, "Only One Life" the famous line: "Only one life, 'twill soon be past, only what's done for Christ will last."

Moved by the accounts of these men's radical obedience

to Christ, I prayed, "Lord, give me the great faith of these men!"

I couldn't have imagined at the time just how important —and how strategic—that prayer would turn out to be.

These men totally trusted in God to provide all that they needed. They had no doubt that God was in control. But their faith went beyond the mere fact that "God can" and went all the way to the unwavering belief that "God will." He *will* do the impossible to advance His kingdom through obedient servants!

After we returned home, I began taking radical steps of faith and obedience. The first thing I did was to apply for seminary at Emory University—to start the program in the upcoming fall quarter—even though I had no way to pay the tuition. Besides that, attending seminary meant I would have to quit a very good job as a programmer analyst.

Still, I trusted that God would provide. After all, His Word says, "My God will supply all your needs according to His riches in glory in Christ Jesus" (Philippians 4:19 NASB) and also, "Nothing will be impossible with God" (Luke 1:37 NASB). I had learned these Scriptures. I had read testimonies regarding the application of those Scriptures. Now it was time for me to put them into practice!

We put our house up for sale and it was not a normal situation at all. First of all, the builder who developed our neighborhood had gone bankrupt right in the middle of building our house and the ones beside us. In fact, we had to buy our house on the courthouse steps just six months prior. It was unfinished at the time, and several suppliers had not been paid yet.

So we had to buy the house, pay the suppliers, and then finish it ourselves. At this point, we had finished everything except parts of the basement, and we did not have time to finish it before we needed to sell. We would have to sell quickly in order for me to be able to pay for seminary.

Besides the fact that our house was not completely finished, there sat around our house several other unfinished houses. And to top it all off, the US had been in a nearly two-year recession.

Like these men of great faith, Belinda and I sought to be totally led by the Lord. We did not list the house with a real estate agent. We didn't even put a "For Sale" sign in the front yard. Rather, we simply got direction to put an ad in the newspaper, and within a very short time, we got a full-price offer on our house. The closing happened very quickly, and we walked away with a 50% profit on the sale of our home after only six months of living there.

God knew our need, and He was showing us that we could trust Him.

In late August, I quit my job and started seminary.

By December of 1975, I had already finished my first quarter of seminary. We got invited by Jack and Kay to go on a tour of the Holy Land in Israel along with my parents, and my parents graciously paid for all of our expenses. Everything was moving so quickly and working out so well.

A new direction for our lives was beginning to unfold—a direction that would eventually impact hundreds of thousands for Christ—all because I had prayed, "Lord, I will be anything you want me to be, go anywhere you want me to go, and do anything you want me to do!" and then later, "Lord, give me the great faith of these men!"

What about you? What's next in your life? If you're not sure, just pray, "Lord, I'll do anything you want me to do." Pray "Lord, give me great faith!" and then believe Him to do the impossible. You just might start an adventure that will impact many for Christ!

6

I AM SERIOUS—I NEED YOUR HELP!

Once I was obedient to enroll in seminary, got accepted, and paid my tuition, I still had a problem. I had never learned to study! Yes, I had a degree from the University of Georgia. But my grades were not that great. I enjoyed the night life too much while I was a student there.

When I met Belinda around the start of my junior year, my grades did improve significantly. But I still never learned how to study effectively. Besides that, I had been out of college for five years at this point. Now here I was, all set to pursue a Master of Divinity degree at Emory University! Not an easy task!

I caught a major break when my academic advisor enrolled me in several easy courses for my first quarter in the MDiv program. I worked as hard as I could and got all A's that first quarter. Through that result, God blessed me with an academic scholarship for the remainder of my first year.

During the second quarter, I got into some tougher classes. Now I really needed some help in effective studying. What I had been doing up to that point was very time-consuming, and definitely not the best method. Because I had no idea how to take notes or study properly, I had come up with a process that involved me recording each lecture on a tape recorder. Then I would go home and write out the entire lecture word for word.

After we moved into an apartment, I used the second bedroom as an office for studying and doing schoolwork. One night, I sat reviewing the written notes I had made from a recent lecture. But nothing was coming together.

So I just kept praying and asking God to help me learn the material. But for some reason, it just wasn't happening. After a while, I walked into the living room and found Belinda.

"I need help. Can we pray together?" I asked.

She said, "Sure, what's the matter?"

I just said, "Can you please come into the bedroom and pray with me?"

We went into the bedroom and knelt down. I explained to Belinda what was going on, and we began to pray together. At this point, I was feeling very desperate, so my prayer was earnest. "Lord, I am serious! I need your help!"

Belinda prayed for me and then went back into the living room. I retook my seat in the office and began reviewing the material again. The rest of the night was completely different from that point on. The material began to make sense to me. It was all coming together. I had a great study session, and then Belinda and I went to bed together. I didn't have to pull an all-nighter or anything.

The next morning I went to school, took the test, and made an A!

There had been so much pressure on me up until that point. I had resigned from my job and we had sold our house. I was pursuing a master's degree at a difficult university. All of this represented a completely new and unexpected direction for our lives. And everything had moved very fast.

It felt like so much was riding on my ability to do well in this program.

What I learned that day was that when God promises in His Word to supply all of our needs according to His riches in glory in Christ Jesus, He's not just promising to meet our financial and physical needs. He's promising to meet all of our needs. All.

I really needed to be able to understand this material. On my own, I couldn't do it. I wasn't getting there. But God saw the need and supplied for it out of His riches in glory.

After all, He made me. He designed every human mind that ever existed. He knows exactly how to supply whatever the need is, whether it is physical, mental, emotional, relational—you name it. Is there someone you need to get connected with? Do you need God's favor to come through another person? God can do it!

Do you need emotional healing?

God can supply it!

Not only can He supply your need, He will! God

delights in supplying for our needs. All of them. Whatever you need, just ask Him right now. And trust that He will answer.

I declare to you today that whatever you need, *in His plan for you,* it is yours in Christ!

7

READY OR NOT, HERE I COME!

God was so extremely good and faithful to me during my time in seminary. With His help, I received an academic scholarship throughout all three years. I graduated with Cum Laude honors and received my Master of Divinity degree in June 1978. Shortly after, I got my first ministry position as the associate pastor of First United Methodist Church in Winder, Georgia. Everything seemed to be lining up for us, but life still felt very incomplete.

At this point, Belinda and I had been married for nine years, and we had tried everything to get pregnant. We had gone to doctors and fertility specialists and had done all the things they recommended. Every attempt seemed to fail miserably. Belinda really began to have her heart set on adoption, but I was not open to the idea.

Then in December of '78, my parents saw an ad in a church bulletin. It read, "Baby for Adoption" and there was a phone number. Belinda wanted to at least call and see where it might lead, so I agreed.

It turned out that the phone number was to a law office. The attorney was representing a young lady who wanted to give up her baby for adoption, but she had certain requirements in mind. She wanted to live with the family during the time of her pregnancy, be supported by them, and get to know them. She also wanted the family to financially support her for several months after the baby was born.

We did not have the funds to pursue this adoption, and we ultimately turned the opportunity down. It was a pretty tough decision for Belinda, because she really wanted a baby. All she could think was, *All this time, we've been praying for a baby, and now here is one we can have!* However, after much prayer, we just didn't believe it was God's will for us to pursue this particular adoption.

Shortly after making this decision, Belinda felt heartbroken. She came to a place of surrender, and with a very heavy heart, she knelt down and prayed, "Lord, if you never want me to have children, I accept this!"

But I was now much more open to the idea of adoption. Not long after this all took place, I was praying and asking for direction about whether or not to adopt. I felt that I heard the Lord speaking and answering me. This is the message that came to me in prayer that day:

God adopted you, so you do likewise.
Each child is My creation.

If I use you, or another to bring My child into the world,

then I will select the parents.

All are Mine.

I entrust them to you.

I wrote down the message and showed it to Belinda, then said confidently, "We are supposed to adopt."

She was happy, but cautious about getting her hopes up. After all, the previous opportunity to adopt was no longer available. We didn't have any real plan or prospects—all we had was a word. We had direction from God to adopt, but with no funds available to do so, all we could do was wait on Him.

Several months later, we were sitting at home on a Saturday night. The phone rang. This was long before the days of caller ID, but when the phone was still ringing, I said, "That is someone calling about adoption." I wasn't even sure where the words came from. I just knew.

Belinda answered and there was a lady on the other end. She explained, "You don't know me. I don't know you either. But I understand you are interested in adoption."

Belinda confirmed that we were, and the lady went on to explain that there was a pregnant teen who had been forced to leave home. A Christian couple had let her come and live with them. The girl had been considering abortion, but this couple convinced her instead to put the baby up for adoption.

So now there was a search underway for parents who would be good candidates to adopt. The lady asked us to write out our Christian beliefs and send them to a liaison who was involved in the search process.

We found it quite challenging to try to explain our Christian beliefs to a teenage girl. But we did our best and mailed the paper to the liaison. The liaison turned out to be another lady who was friends with the Christian couple. She also happened to be friends with the lawyer that Belinda and I had spoken with several months prior!

The liaison told the attorney about her involvement in this young lady's adoption process, and he had recommended for them to contact us. After reading the statement about our beliefs, the teenage girl chose us to be the adoptive parents for her baby.

We were beyond thrilled!

The baby was due to be born in April of 1979. We would soon have a child of our own to parent! We were so excited!

This was before the days of internet, YouTube, and endless information at our fingertips. Back then, if you wanted information about how to take care of a baby, you asked your doctor. So in March of '79, Belinda and I scheduled an appointment with her OB-GYN to find out what we needed to do. How do we prepare? What do we do when we bring our new baby home?

The doctor did a routine examination where he also addressed our questions about taking care of a baby. At one point, he left for quite a while and then came back into the room. But now he was turning the tables on us by asking us some questions.

He looked at Belinda and asked pointedly, "If you got pregnant, would you still adopt this baby?"

She replied, "Yes, of course. This is God's baby for us!"

Then the doctor turned to me. "Ron, if Belinda got pregnant, would you still adopt?"

"Yes, of course. We would still adopt!" I replied.

"Good, because you all are pregnant and the baby is due in October!"

Around the end of April, we got a phone call on a Thursday morning. The person said, "Congratulations! You have a boy!"

As associate pastor, I only preached a few times each year. But I was scheduled to preach that very next Sunday, and my sermon was aptly titled, "Ready or not, here I come!"

Right after church that morning, we went and picked up our first child. Five and a half months later, Belinda gave birth to our second child.

In very short order, we had gone from having no real prospects for becoming parents to having double blessings. And it all started the moment Belinda said, "Lord, if you never want me to have children, I accept this."

Letting go and surrendering completely is not a sign of weakness, but of strength. It takes courage to lay everything at the Lord's feet, ready to accept whatever answer He gives.

The Bible tells us to trust in the Lord with all of our heart, and to lean not on our own understanding. In all of our ways, we are to acknowledge Him, and He will direct our paths.

What can you lay down at God's feet right now? Is it possible that the Lord has a different plan than the one you expect?

Are you ready to accept His plan?

"Ready or not, here I come!"

8

THE YOUTH DID WHAT?

During my time as associate pastor, I was asked to serve on the local county's newly formed "Drug and Alcohol Prevention Committee." One of my major responsibilities on the committee was to create events which would address the problem of drug and alcohol use among the young people in our county.

During the months of May, June, and July of 1980, I created what I called "YouthQuake." I was envisioning a movement among our youth. We had large banners made up which stretched across the main street running through the middle of town.

The first event was planned for early May, before summer break started. The original idea was to invite a Teen Challenge singing group to come and speak at one of the local churches. Teen Challenge is a ministry that helps young people break free of drug and alcohol addiction by turning to Jesus. So the members of the singing group all have testimonies of how Jesus had set them free.

But as I prayed about the event, I felt like God was saying that many young people would not come to a church, so we should have the event in the local high school stadium instead. This felt like a very risky proposition. A public high school? Former drug addicts? I honestly thought that if things went bad, I might lose my job.

Still, it felt like the right plan, so we got it scheduled and then I spent several weeks training the youth of our church on how to present the gospel. We planned to have an altar call at the event, and if people came forward, our youth would be there, waiting to lead them through a salvation prayer!

Belinda was staying home with our two very young children, but she prayed with me before I left that night. I remember telling her, "Belinda, tonight the Lord is going to be glorified or the people of our town are going to tar and feather me!"

The stage was set. The stadium lights were on. And teenagers began to show up in groups. Then more came. Then more.

Even parents were showing up. People poured in until the entire home side of the bleachers was completely full. Besides that, there were many young people hanging out in the parking lot, sitting on the hoods of their cars, just waiting to hear what was going to come out of the speakers.

The Teen Challenge group came out and began to sing songs about Jesus, and the crowd was into it. The teenagers really enjoyed the music! After a while, the group members began to share their testimonies in between songs. One of the members, who had been in a gang, told how he had watched a member of a different gang slit his sister's throat. His story really got the attention of everyone in the crowd, but the most shocking part was when he explained how Jesus had empowered him to completely forgive the man who murdered his sister.

Several more testimonies were shared, and then came a clear, brief presentation of the gospel from the leader of the Teen Challenge group. Then he prayed and invited everyone to come forward and receive Jesus as Lord and Savior. As he was giving the invitation, the sound of the crowd responding sounded like a herd of buffalo making their way down the stands toward the stage.

The YouthQuake was happening!

The young people from our church led more than 200 other teens in salvation prayers that night. No one lost their jobs. All of my worries were unfounded. God amazingly blessed our efforts, and many teenagers received Jesus.

We had a variety of events throughout the summer for our YouthQuake. There was a movie night with The Cross and the Switchblade, which is based on the true story of David Wilkerson and Nicky Cruz. A local theater owner offered up a theater free of charge. We handed out tickets for the event all over town, and it was completely packed.

There was a bonfire at our church. We ate together and had one of the football coaches from the University of Georgia as a guest speaker. At the bonfire, the youth began to bring forward some things they brought with them. Apparently, they had preplanned to get rid of things like records, books, Dungeons and Dragons games, and Ouija boards by throwing them into the fire!

I had not been aware of their plan. It was just something they came up with on their own.

Some people standing near said they had never been around a fire that burned so hot. I don't know if it burned hotter or not, but I know that it had a huge impact on our youth!

Later, as I told people of the night's events, several stopped me and asked, "The youth did what!?!" People were amazed that the youth would take it upon themselves to do something like this, without even a suggestion from any adult. The parents were delighted, and began quickly reporting changes in their teenagers.

It all started when I listened to the Lord and decided to take a risk. I had fears and reservations about bringing "former drug addicts" and gang members to speak at a huge community event. It didn't feel completely safe or comfortable to hold a Christian event at a public school facility.

In Matthew chapter 14, the Bible tells us about a time when the disciples were in a boat on the Sea of Galilee in the middle of the night. Jesus was not with them. All of a sudden, they saw someone walking toward them on the water.

Thinking it was a ghost, they were completely terrified. They cried out in fear, but Jesus said, "Take courage, it is I; do not be afraid."

One of the disciples decided to take him up on that first

part. Peter responded, "Lord, if it is You, command me to come to You on the water."

Jesus said, "Come!"

The other disciples were probably thinking, *Who does Peter think he is? Does he think he can walk on water? This weekend at the Fisherman's Club, we'll be having a great laugh about this!*

But Peter stepped out and he walked on the water too.

Following Christ might mean taking risks that others deem foolish. It can sometimes cost everything to follow Christ. Other times there will be uncertainty, and the situation will feel like it *might* cost us everything.

But if we want to see God's miracles, we have to be willing to follow Him wherever He leads. Are you willing to pray and step out in faith? God may be calling you out of your comfort zone, but if you go, you might see Him do the impossible!

Keep your focus on Jesus, and you will not sink.

9

GIVE AWAY ALL THE MONEY!

During that same year, 1980, our youth was raising money for an upcoming retreat. We had already raised a substantial sum, but we were still shy of the full amount we needed, so we planned a Wash-A-Thon. Our Wash-A-Thon would be held on Saturday morning for four hours, and it would be free to the community.

If someone came up and wanted a car wash, we would gladly do it for them at no charge. Prior to the event, each young person was asked to find supporters who would donate a certain amount of money for each car that we washed. Using this strategy, it looked like we would be able to raise a large sum of money in a very short time.

With the Wash-A-Thon scheduled for the next Saturday, and quite a few people already pledging financial support, we had our normal Sunday evening youth chapel service. That night I asked the young people, "What do you want to be known for as a group? Do you want to be known as one who is always asking for money? Or would you rather be known as a group that is serving the community for Christ?"

Next, I shared several stories with them about those missionaries I mentioned before who had always trusted the Lord to provide for their needs—George Mueller, Hudson Taylor, C.T. Studd. We talked about Scriptures like Philippians 4:19, "And my God will supply all your needs according to His riches in glory in Christ Jesus."

The youth began to talk about this topic, both among themselves and with the youth leaders as well. Before long, the youth had decided that they wanted to be known as a group that served its community for Christ. Not long after that, one young person spoke up and said, "Let's give away all the money we have raised for the summer trip! We can use it to help others in this community!"

Many of the young people were in agreement, with some adding, "Let's pray that God will supply all of our needs for the upcoming retreat!"

Upon hearing this, I told the young people, "This is what we are going to do. The counselors and I will leave the chapel and you all remain here. This is a very important decision, and I want you all to discuss it among yourselves. I'm going to leave these index cards out. After you discuss this, take some quiet time so each of you can pray individually about it as well. Then, when you're ready, write down what you think we should do on an index card—keep the money, give away some of the money, or give away all of the money. After you write down your decision, leave your index card on the altar. When everyone is finished, come and get us."

Before walking out I reminded them, "If you choose to give away all of the money, there is no other money available to pay for the upcoming trip!"

After about 15 minutes, one of the young people came and told us they were finished. We walked in and I collected all of the index cards into a neat stack, and then I began reading them one by one.

"Give away all of the money."

"Give it all away!"

"Give it all away for Jesus!"

My heart raced as I read through each of the 48 cards. Finally, there was only one left. I thought surely this wouldn't be a unanimous decision, before turning it over.

"Give away all of the money."

I couldn't believe it. My next thought was, *This decision is going to have a major impact on the lives of these youth and their faith in Jesus! Not only that,* I thought, *this is also going to impact their parents, other church members, staff, and the community!*

Then questions and doubts began to arise.

Have I truly listened to the Lord here, and led the youth in the way He wants us to go?

Quickly, I silenced that concern, thinking, *Well,* there's no turning back now. The decision has been made by the youth!

Next, I told the group what we would do. We would print a slip of paper explaining the youth's decision and they would take it to the people who had pledged support for the Wash-A-Thon. Instead of giving us financial support, we were now asking them to "pray for us according to Philippians 4:19, that God will supply all of our needs according to His riches in glory in Christ Jesus."

Once the youth took these slips of paper to explain our decision to those who had pledged financial support, the word got out. The youth's decision quickly became the talk of the town!

The Wash-A-Thon took place as scheduled the very next Saturday. It was a completely free event with no financial backing—just an opportunity for the youth to serve without getting anything in return. A handful of people still put a dollar or two in the buckets that were lying around, but it didn't amount to much money. We figured God had some other plan for providing, but what would it be? No one knew.

The money previously raised by the youth was now being given away to various causes and groups in our community who were in need. With each donation, we explained that it was a gift from our youth group, and that we were thankful for the opportunity to help.

As the word spread throughout the community about what the youth were doing, the church office began to receive checks designated for our youth. This had never happened before.

Normally when people donate to a church, they just make out a check to the church with no specifications about where the money will go, unless maybe the church has some specific fundraiser set up. In this case, we weren't asking for anything, but people were giving!

The checks kept coming. And coming. And coming. More and more money poured in. During this time, the youth were meeting regularly at the church to pray that God would supply all of our needs according to His riches in glory in Christ Jesus.

We were still very short of what we needed for the upcoming trip, but excitement was building. The youth kept praying.

Finally, we came upon a deadline. We had only one week to come up with the remaining amount and book the trip, or we would have to cancel. I was set to attend a men's meeting at the church that night. With the money we already had, we still needed $542 to be able to book the trip.

That afternoon, my parents called. Dad was a captain with Eastern Airlines, and he was explaining that they had sent him a bonus check that was completely unexpected. It was more than enough to cover the remaining amount we needed to book our trip, and they wanted to donate the money to our youth!

With a bit of a sigh, I responded, "Thank you so much. That is incredibly generous, but I can't accept it. If I accept the money from you, people will think that I just called my parents to get the needed funds, and God will not get the glory He should get from this. I'm going to have to decline the donation. God will make another way."

It was a very difficult thing to say, but I really believed God would make another way.

That night, at the men's meeting, one of the men came up and started talking to me. He explained, "I have property that generates income. I really don't need the money, and I would like to donate the income to the youth."

This man had never given money to the youth before. I said, "Okay, are you wanting to support the upcoming trip?"

"What trip?"

"The youth have an upcoming trip. They raised most of the money for it, and then they gave it away—" I began explaining.

He interrupted, "No. I just had this money and the thought came to me to donate it to the youth."

I was encouraged. God was moving! The man handed me a sealed envelope that felt like it was full of cash. I thanked him for his donation, but I didn't think it was appropriate to ask him how much it was or to open the envelope.

When I got back home that night, I told Belinda about what happened, and we opened the envelope together. We counted the money, and with a mixture of shock, disbelief, and ecstatic joy, we counted it again.

It was $542!

This man had no idea what had been going on with the youth. Besides that, I had not shared the latest balance of funds with anyone.

Belinda and I were beyond excited! We fell to our knees and thanked God for supplying all of the youth group's needs—and doing it in His perfect way! Not too early, but definitely not too late!

I called one of the youth counselors and told him what happened. He called a few of the youth and some of the other counselors. The story began spreading like wildfire.

During those weeks after the youth decided to give away all of their money, so many people in the community wondered whether they would get the money they needed in the end. They did, but that wasn't the important part of what took place.

What really mattered is that the youth took a step of faith, and they were able to experience firsthand the faithfulness of God. They had discussed it among themselves. They had prayed over the matter, seeking the Lord's direction. And they were obedient to His direction.

Our youth believed God for what seemed impossible. They believed God to supply their needs without asking anyone else. The lives of the youth were never the same. They had indeed experienced the living God.

To this day, all these years later, some of those (formerly) young people still talk about what a special time that was in their lives.

What about you—what do you want to be known for?

Do you want to be known as a person who loves God and loves people? Do you want to be known as a person who is always asking for things, or a person who is always giving of themselves?

Whatever situation you're dealing with right now, ask God for a way to turn it around. Ask Him for a way to make it about Him and His glory.

And then be obedient to His direction.

He will not disappoint!

10

NEVER AGAIN

In June of 1981, I was given the opportunity to become the senior pastor of First United Methodist Church in Adairsville, Georgia. Whenever you are the senior pastor of a small or medium-sized church, one of your primary duties during the week is visiting sick members of your congregation in the local hospital.

This one particular time, in 1981, I was going to the hospital to visit a congregant who was in for surgery, and a member of our church asked if I would go by and visit their friend, who happened to be in the same hospital.

I went by to see the man and visited with him for a while. We talked about the weather, sports, world events— pretty much everything you can think of except Christianity.

Later on, I heard that the man had died while in the hospital. I did not know the man's spiritual condition, and in the weeks that followed, it weighed on me that I had not asked him.

Sometime later, in that same hospital, I was again visiting a church member's sick friend. I went by to see the man and we talked about weather, sports, world events— pretty much everything you can think of except Christianity.

Leaving the man's room, I walked to the elevator and pressed the button. The door opened and I stepped inside. As the door began to close, something rose up in me.

"Never again!" I said to myself before hurriedly finding the "Open" button. *I will never again be too embarrassed or uncomfortable to share the gospel!*

I walked briskly back to the man's room before stopping right outside to pray. I said, "Lord, help me to talk to this man about you. If he does not know you, I pray that he will come to know you as Lord and Savior today!"

Stepping back into the man's hospital room, my mind was now completely fixed on eternal matters. I did not know him before that day, but I cared about this man. I cared where he would spend eternity.

As we talked, I asked for his permission to ask him some questions about himself. Then I explained that my aim was for him to be able to know beyond any doubt that he would go to Heaven if he died. He gave his permission, and I began to share the gospel with him.

Once I finished explaining the gospel, I asked the man if he would like to pray and receive Jesus as his Lord and Savior, and he very much wanted that. We prayed together, and the man received Christ that day.

What about you? Is there anything for which you have said, "Never again"? Are you willing to make the decision now to stand by that promise in the future? Or will you be swayed by others' perception of you?

When I reentered that man's hospital room, I thought, *God, You love this man more than I ever could. You will give me the words to say, as long as I am willing to say them.* The same is true for you any time you feel compelled to share the gospel.

In the moments when you fear rejection or discomfort, I encourage you to stand strong in your conviction and rely on God for the rest. It could very well make the difference in someone's eternal destination!

11

LORD, I JUST NEED TO HEAR A WORD FROM YOU

At First United Methodist Church, we held regular Bible study meetings throughout the week. One night in 1982, I was at one such meeting when I shared a story about a missionary who was sick and in need of prayer.

The other missionaries were going to pray for him, but before they could begin praying, the leader made a request of them. He asked them to return home and ask God if there was anything in their lives that they needed to confess. Then, they were to ask the Lord (or offended person) to forgive them. When they gathered at the next meeting, they would then pray for the healing of the sick missionary.

There was a man in our group named Tommy who had been suffering from severe back pain. So I asked our Bible study group to do the same as the leader from my story—to go home and confess their sin and ask for forgiveness before returning to pray for his healing.

When I went back to my own home, I said, "God, whatever it takes to bring this community to You, do it." I had no idea what was about to happen next!

A few days later, Belinda became very sick with flu-like symptoms. I took her to the emergency room at Redmond Regional Medical Center in Rome, Georgia. The doctor gave her a prescription and sent us home. But Belinda did not get better.

Two days later I took her back to the hospital emergency room, where this time she was admitted. I was deeply concerned, so I called an internal medicine doctor we knew at Piedmont Hospital in Atlanta. He requested Belinda be transferred there by ambulance.

As I was driving to meet her there, I heard a voice in my spirit say, "She is going to die." At the time, Belinda was just thirty-two years old. Timothy, our son we adopted, was three, and Ann Marie, the daughter Belinda carried, was two-and-a-half. Belinda had too much to live for. I would not accept death as her fate.

"In the name of Jesus," I prayed out loud, "and through the blood of Jesus, I command Satan and your evil powers to be bound." Immediately, the voice went away. About a half hour later, it returned. Again, I repeated the same command and the voice was silenced.

When I arrived at the emergency room, I learned that Belinda had deteriorated so quickly that they had placed her in the intensive care unit. I asked the doctor, "What do you think the problem is?"

The doctor shrugged. "It could be spinal meningitis, leukemia, or . . . something else. We really don't know."

At that moment, I decided to use a system for processing information. Unless a doctor came to me with absolute confirmation of any fact, I would not even think about it as a possibility.

Multiple doctors evaluated Belinda's condition, but no diagnosis could be determined. She continued to grow increasingly worse until she was placed on life support. She was slipping away rapidly, falling in and out of consciousness.

We continued to fight for Belinda in our spirits. Our church held a prayer vigil around the clock. I reached out to Jack and Kay Arthur too. Kay asked her staff around the world to pray that Belinda would be healed.

My dad did calligraphy, so I asked him to write down several Scriptures that had come to mind: "For with God nothing shall be impossible" (Luke 1:37 KJV), ". . . for the joy of the Lord is your strength" (Nehemiah 8:10 KJV), "For we walk by faith, not by sight" (2 Corinthians 5:7 KJV), "But my God shall supply all your need according to his riches in glory by Christ Jesus" (Philippians 4:19 KJV), and, "I can do all things through Christ which strengtheneth me" (Philippians 4:13 KJV).

We placed the beautifully-written Scriptures all around Belinda's room. Throughout the day, I would read them out loud to her. Though she wasn't alert, I was filling the room with the Word of God.

Despite all of our efforts with prayer and faith, Belinda's condition grew even more serious. I felt that I needed to get out of the hospital—to be alone with God. So I took my Bible and got in the passenger seat of my car, thinking, *No one will think I'm trying to move my car if I'm sitting over here. They won't be waiting on my parking space!* I knew the discussion God and I were about to have might take some time.

With my Bible in my lap, I prayed the most difficult and heart-wrenching prayer I've ever prayed. I said out loud, "God, if You want to take Belinda home to be with You, then do it." Then I experienced the worst feeling I have ever felt. I felt like I was in the pit of hell—there was such an emptiness. Then I prayed, "But God, I do not think that is what You want. Lord, I just need to hear a Word from You! Please give me the Scripture to show me what You are going to do."

I opened my Bible and began flipping through it. I stopped on a specific page and my finger moved down the left column and stopped. I was on Acts 3:16: "And on the basis of faith in His name, *it is* the name of Jesus which has strengthened this man whom you see and know; and the faith which comes through Him, has given him this perfect health, in the presence of you all" (NASB). My heart leaped with joy!

I read the Scripture again, putting Belinda's name in the place of "man." "And on the basis of faith in His name, it is the name of Jesus which has strengthened Belinda whom you see and know; and the faith which comes through Jesus, has given Belinda this perfect health, in the presence of you all."

I kept reading the verse out loud, over and over again. My faith grew stronger and stronger. I had such confidence. *God is going to heal Belinda!* Acts 3:16 had been God's confirmation to me!

I opened the glove box in the car and found several blank index cards. Taking my pen, I started writing the Scripture down. As I wrote, I read out loud. When I had gotten in the car, I had been empty. But now, I felt full of strength in the Lord's presence and promise.

I left the car and went back into the hospital. I took the index cards and my Bible with me. I went straight to Belinda's room and taped one of those cards on the tray beside her bed. Though Belinda was not conscious, I read it out loud to Belinda, using her name.

That Friday afternoon the doctor said he didn't know if Belinda would make it through the night. I called one of the leaders of our church and said, "This Sunday is to be a praise service. Tell the congregation that no matter what happens, we are to praise God in and for all situations."

Everyone continued praying for Belinda, who miraculously made it through Friday night alive. By Saturday morning, though, nothing had changed. Even the CDC had tried to determine what was wrong, but they, too, had no answers.

That morning a new doctor came by Belinda's room. I hadn't met this doctor before. In passing, he mentioned he was teaching Sunday school the following day.

"What's your topic?" I asked him.

"Acts chapter three," he replied.

I almost shouted right there in the intensive care unit! Instead, I said, "Come back and see Belinda again. I will tell you a story to add to your teaching on Acts chapter three."

On Sunday morning a new day dawned. Seemingly out of nowhere, Belinda's vitals began to improve. Then, little by little, Belinda became alert. She even started talking! Before we knew it, we were moved out of intensive care into a private room.

A day or two later, one of the intensive care nurses who had taken care of Belinda came to visit. She said, "All of a sudden, it was like you decided to live!"

Belinda said, "I was lying in bed and heard a voice say, 'You have not been a good mother and a good wife. You deserve to die!'" (Which absolutely was not true, Belinda had been a wonderful mother and wife!) Belinda thought about what she heard and responded, "That is not true! I have been a good mother and a good wife, and I am not afraid to die!"

What happened next in Belinda's body, only God knows. But He healed her, just like He showed me he would. Sunday morning was a praise service, indeed!

Several weeks before Belinda went into the hospital, a local high school had asked me to speak at their baccalaureate service and in the school. The night Belinda came home from the hospital, I gave the baccalaureate address. The next week, I spoke to the students at the school for several days, sharing our testimony and the gospel with them. During those few days, over two hundred high school students placed their trust in Jesus Christ as their Lord and Savior.

You may remember that at the beginning of this story I had prayed, "God, whatever it will take to bring this community to You, do it!" Well, that's what happened! But God wasn't finished performing miracles yet.

After being home for several weeks, we received several

medical bills from Redmond Hospital, Piedmont Hospital, and the doctors. One of the Scriptures we had put up on the wall in Belinda's room was, "My God shall supply all your needs according to His riches in glory in Christ Jesus" (Philippians 4:19, NASB).

Our insurance had paid part of the bills, but not all of them. We began praying, asking the Lord to help supply the money to pay the outstanding balances. One day I went to the mailbox and found an envelope from the IRS. I opened the envelope, and inside was a check written for the exact amount of the remaining medical bills. We were pleasantly surprised!

It was not a refund from past taxes, so I called the IRS to find out what the check was for. "We received a check from you. We do not know why. What are we supposed to do?"

There was silence on the other end of the phone. The agent asked several questions, then told me to wait. Some time passed, and the agent returned. "Cash it!" she said.

We did, and paid all the remaining bills!

When all seems to be crashing in on you, where do you turn? Do you rely on your own wisdom and strength? Or the wisdom and strength of men?

You see, we had faithful friends, medical staff, and family standing with us, but even they were not enough. Far above everything else, our wisdom and strength has always come from the Lord.

Whatever you are facing today, He is waiting for you to allow Him to walk through it with you. I had prayed, "Lord, I just need to hear a word from You!" He answered, and I received, accepted, believed, and trusted what He said.

Are you ready to ask, then wait and listen? He is prepared to give you the wisdom and strength you need to face anything!

12

17 DAYS TO VICTORY

Two years later in 1984, our family was still in Adairsville at FUMC, and our congregation was in the middle of a building project. We were constructing our Family Life Center, which included classrooms, a nursery, an office, a fellowship hall, and a kitchen.

The project was about 70 percent complete at this time, but several large invoices were coming due in the next 17 days, and we were running out of money. Prior to breaking ground, our church had voted *not* to take on a loan for the project.

People were saying, "We've given all we can. What else can we do?"

In my mind I thought, *Now the Lord has us exactly where He wants us to be.* Because I knew that it's in situations like these, when we can only rely on God to provide, that He is able to accomplish the impossible.

So I preached a sermon called "17 Days to Victory,"

and announced that our administrative council would meet at the end of that time period to determine whether or not we should reverse our previous decision about borrowing money. My message called on the congregation to pray and seek God's direction.

The sanctuary was open daily, and I placed a paper at the altar that listed God's promises from the Bible. I wanted to encourage people to look to the Lord, to ask *Him* what He wanted us to do. I also left a stack of index cards and pens at the altar and asked people to write down what they felt the Lord spoke to them during their prayer time. Then, I asked them to leave the cards at the altar.

During those 17 days, people came to the church to pray. Belinda and I prayed too. Beyond our budgeted tithe, we asked God what He'd want us to give. I felt God was prompting us to sell our Ford Mustang, so I drove it to the dealership and asked the owner, "How much will you give me for my car?" He tried to talk me out of it, but I asked him again, "How much is it worth to you?"

The evening of the 17th day came. I was irritated when I left Belinda and the kids at home to go to the church for the final decision. "I have had it with these people," I sadly and wrongly told her. It felt as if everyone has been grumbling and complaining.

Before the vote was taken, I stood and expressed my belief that it is not best to borrow money to build God's facilities. I sat down and the chairman of the council explained our reason for meeting. Then he asked the group, "What do you want to do?"

Someone stood up. Instead of talking about how to vote,

he surprised me by saying, "My family is prepared to give." Then he specified an amount. Then another person stood up and shared the amount their family could give. I felt led to stand and say, "Belinda and I will give our Ford Mustang. The dealership owner said he would buy my car at this amount."

All around the room, individuals and couples began calling out dollar amounts they could give that week. It was like a bingo game, numbers being recited in rapid fire. This went on for some time!

One of our members yelled out, "How much more money do we need?"

I had been adding up the amounts as quickly as possible. I gave him the answer, "Fifteen hundred dollars."

"That's mine," someone said.

But it didn't stop there. More dollar amounts were pledged, far beyond what we needed. The voice of one very "proper" elderly lady rang out, "I could run down Main Street, praising God!"

After the meeting was complete, several of the men came up to me and said, "Ron, we have more money than we need. You don't have to sell your car."

I thanked them, but said, "Belinda and I prayed about it. So tonight, when I said I would give my car, I meant it. We have to stand by our promise to God."

The next morning I drove my Mustang to the Ford dealership with the title in hand. A friend gave me a ride straight to our church treasurer's home to give her the promised check. It didn't feel sad—it felt exciting!

In fact, there was a new energy in the church. We had

the money to pay the upcoming invoices, and even *more* was coming in. The building project was completed and all paid on time.

I was deeply grateful, but Belinda and I were still down to one car. It wasn't impossible, but it wasn't convenient either. However, we resolved not to complain. We knew everything we had belonged to the Lord.

But imagine our shock when one day we pulled into our driveway to find a car in it. And not just a car, but one with a title and keys! It would be *years* before we found out who had donated the car to us, but we had known who our provider was—God.

What about you? Do you have faith that God can and will meet your every need? Are you facing financial challenges right now? Will you believe that God can take your "impossible" situation and work it out for His glory?

Yes, we experienced victory at the end of our 17 days, but it ran so much deeper than money. The money is what God used to get our attention. Could He be trying to get your attention now too?

Will you come to the altar and pray, submitting all your requests to the only One who can meet your deepest needs?

13

GO APPLY!

A small, soft voice spoke to me, "Go apply."

Les, a friend of mine, had mentioned a new organization called The Mission Society for United Methodists. I had never considered being a missionary before, but as I was praying a few days later, a voice persisted: "Go apply."

Years before, at the retreat where Belinda and I met Jack and Kay Arthur, you'll remember I prayed, "God, I will be anything you want me to be. I will go anywhere you want me to go. I will do anything you want me to do." It occurred to me that despite still being the pastor at FUMC, my declaration to God certainly included the possibility of becoming a missionary.

Belinda and I had learned years before to trust God to lead us. We accepted that we may not know why or how, but to do exactly as He told us to do. So I called The Mission

Society and asked them to send an application to our address in Adairsville.

Belinda and I read the information we received, and we each completed our applications. We mailed them off and shortly afterward received a call to come in for an interview.

An interview? I wondered. *For what?*

I soon learned that this was one step in the process to become a missionary—a post which, as I've said, neither Belinda nor I had ever desired to hold. But sure enough, after several interviews, we were accepted as candidates to become missionaries with the organization.

It was a very strange experience for both of us. Here we were, having a successful ministry in the local church, and we'd just become candidates for missionary work. What would our congregation think? *All that matters, I told myself, is that we were obedient to God.*

It wasn't long before The Mission Society offered us a position in Ghana, West Africa. After meeting with the bishop from that area, we prayed. It didn't feel like the right opportunity for us, so we passed. But we did request to remain on the active list for future assignments.

What are you up to, God? I prayed. But His answer didn't come in the form I thought it would—at least not yet.

In my fourth year as pastor of FUMC, I completed the doctoral program at Candler School of Theology at Emory University, earning a Doctor of Ministry degree. Toward the end of my last year of study in 1985, my district superintendent asked if we might consider moving to a new church. After much prayer, we accepted the new position.

Several months before our move, I called The Mission

Society and asked if there was anything available for us, but there was nothing. *What was that all about, God?* I asked. *Why did you ask me to apply?* There was no answer yet, so we moved to Boynton United Methodist Church in Ringgold, Georgia, close to the Tennessee line.

God's promise to me had always been in the back of my mind: *I am going to use you to reach hundreds of thousands of people for Me.* It had been 10 years since God had spoken those words to me, and I still believed He would accomplish them in His time, in His place, and in His way. It wasn't time for us to become missionaries just yet, but God had already accomplished so much in our lives. We did not doubt His faithfulness.

What about you? When God leads you in a new direction, and it doesn't work out exactly the way you thought it would, do you trust that He is still faithful? A still, quiet voice had said to me, "Go apply." What is His voice nudging you to do? Will you be obedient to His calling?

14

WHAT WOULD YOU SAY?

While serving as the pastor at Boynton United Methodist Church, I volunteered to serve part-time as chaplain for the local hospital. One evening, I was on call when the nurse's station contacted me. I left home, drove to Fort Oglethorpe, and went to the nurse's station.

I was told that there was a patient scheduled for surgery the following morning who was quite anxious and asking for a chaplain. Before entering the patient's room, I paused to pray, then I listened. I went inside and began speaking with the lady. In a short time, I had built a significant level of trust with her.

"I want to ask you two important questions," I said. "Have you come to a place in your spiritual life that you know for certain that one day you will go to Heaven?"

"No," she responded.

I then said, "Someday, if you were to stand before God,

and He asks why He should allow you into Heaven, what would you say?"

"I am trusting in Jesus alone, and what He has done for me on the cross."

I knew then that she was a Christian, but she did not yet have assurance of her salvation. So I shared 1 John 5:13 (NASB) with her: "These things I have written to you who believe in the name of the Son of God, so that you may know that you have eternal life."

I then handed her a Bible and showed her the Scripture. I had her read it out loud, replacing "you" with her own name. I listened to her and we spoke a bit more, then we prayed, and I left.

The next day the nurse called and said the patient had been calm after I left and fell asleep without any problems. "Oh," she added, "and the surgery was successful!"

There are times in our lives when we are called to bridge the gap between a person and God. As we pray, we are to listen to God. He will give us the words to meet the person's needs and bring them comfort.

In the Scriptures we read to be still and know that *He* is God. As we wait on Him, God calms our hearts and minds and brings peace into the situation. You do not have to be a pastor. You do not have to know the Bible cover-to-cover. By simply praying and listening to God, He can speak to and through us.

Are you in a situation right now where you need God's words so that you can be empowered to speak to a friend or loved one? Or maybe someone at work or an acquaintance?

God will tell you exactly what to say, and when, if you will pray and listen.

15

GIVE ME MY CHECKBOOK

Once again, I found myself pastoring a church in the middle of a building project. This time, we were building a new sanctuary.

Like at FUMC, Boynton UMC had also decided not to borrow money to complete construction, so we had to have money in the bank to pay the bills. We were expecting our new steeple to be delivered, but the company who had constructed it for us required cash-on-delivery, meaning a check had to be paid to them before they would install the steeple.

After church hours, it was customary for members of our congregation to bring checks by the parsonage where we lived. On Wednesday night, I stopped by the church during choir practice to deliver the checks that had been handed in that afternoon. So far, we did not have enough money to pay for the end-of-week delivery.

I gave the checks to the church treasurer, who was in the choir.

"How much more do we need?" someone asked. Everyone was curious whether we had enough to cover the steeple and its installation. The treasurer did some quick math and then responded with an amount.

The church member who had asked that question stood and said, "Give me my checkbook!" She explained that she had been saving money for a personal project, but that she now wanted to give the full amount to cover the steeple. "My project can wait," she said.

When the crane lifted up the giant steeple to place it on top of the new sanctuary, the lady—who happened to live directly across the street from the church—stood in her front yard, wordlessly grateful, with tears streaming down her face. She praised God, experiencing the joy of the Lord for what He had done in her life, and what He was continuing to do. For her, the gift had come through *giving*.

The theme of the church's building project was, "Building Lives, Not Buildings." The new sanctuary we had constructed was to proclaim the message of a supernatural God to a skeptical world. One of the stained-glass windows installed on the side entrance read, "Through it All." We even made lapel pins for our members to wear with letters on them commemorating the saying. But instead of "t.i.a.," we had the pins read, "i.t.a.," moving the "t" to the center to represent the cross.

At the end of each Sunday service, we sang the song "Through it All." The words are:

Through it all,
Through it all,
I've learned to trust in Jesus.
I've learned to trust in God.
Through it all,
Through it all,
I've learned to depend upon His Word.

A large Chattanooga newspaper covered the story on their front page, along with a picture of the steeple. The title of the article was, "The Church Built on Faith."

Several pastors around the state called me and asked, "How did you do it?"

"I preached about faith and prayer," I said.

"Who did you hire to lead the fundraising?" they asked.

"No one. No financial commitment cards. No pledges."

They couldn't understand. They invited me to come and tell the story. I said, "Instead of me, I'll send a group of members." Who better to talk about God's faithfulness to us —through it all?

In addition to the sanctuary, God—through our congregation—funded new classrooms, offices, a choir room, and a youth center. But this project was about so much more than money. It was about faith and God's provision. It was about remembering what God had already done, and trusting Him with the future. It was about the act of giving becoming the true gift.

Is there a situation in your life right now that might seem like it's about money, but really, it's about having faith through it all?

What do you need to have faith for right now?

Maybe it will help to take a moment and reflect on these verses:

I have shown you in every way, by laboring like this, that you must support the weak. And remember the words of the Lord Jesus, that He said, 'It is more blessed to give than to receive.' "

— ACTS 20:35 NKJV

But seek first the kingdom of God and His righteousness, and all these things shall be added to you.

— MATTHEW 6:33 NKJV

Therefore I say to you, whatever things you ask when you pray, believe that you receive them, and you will have them.

— MARK 11:24 NKJV

16

THIS IS IT!

While still pastoring at Boynton in the late 1980s, our phone rang.

"This is Dr. Lajara," the caller informed me. "I am the Executive Vice President of Evangelism Explosion International."

It was like someone pulled a chain attached to a light bulb. I thought, *This is it! This is how the Lord will accomplish what He promised to do twelve years ago when He called me into ministry. This is how He is going to use me to reach hundreds of thousands for Him!*

"I've heard about your ministry in the local church over the last few years," Dr. Lajara explained. "Have you ever considered going to Africa as missionaries?"

He went on to say that his organization had recently created a vice president position that would oversee Evangelism Explosion's ministry throughout all 53 nations of Africa, *and* he wanted to know if Belinda and I would come to a meeting to discuss the possibility of me taking that position. Belinda and I both agreed that we should accept the meeting.

After that initial meeting with Dr. Lajara, Belinda and I were invited to Fort Lauderdale, Florida, to meet with Evangelism Explosion President, Dr. D. James Kennedy, and their board of directors. They flew us there, and even invited us to stay the weekend. But Belinda and I declined to stay that long. We were in the middle of our large construction project in Boynton, and our congregation had no idea that three years prior, we had applied to be missionaries—an endeavor we'd put on hold until now.

We had our apprehensions, especially Belinda. She didn't want to move our family to Africa. Besides that, our church was thriving. We'd even won Church of the Year from our district. It would be incredibly difficult to share with them any plans of our leaving. But both of us were willing to listen, to be obedient to the Lord's call. In my spirit I felt, *This is it!*

During our conversation with the board, Belinda said, "I do not know a man of God who has greater faith than Ron."

I shot her a look. *I thought she didn't want to go to Africa.* But her words, spoken from her heart, moved me. I had already shared with her, "If this doesn't work out, if this isn't what the Lord wants us to do, then forget the overseas mission field. I will remain a pastor."

After our discussions with both Dr. Kennedy and the board, we were asked to step out of the conference room to allow them time to talk. We did, and after a short time, we were invited back in.

Dr. Kennedy said, "We'd like to offer you the position of Vice President of Evangelism Explosion for the continent of Africa."

I thanked the board and Dr. Kennedy and said, "Belinda and I would like to pray about this decision. If accepted, it would greatly impact our life and our children's lives. I will get back to you with our answer."

We returned home and prayed, as promised. It felt like we were living in two different worlds. We couldn't discuss our situation with any of our church members, and I felt overwhelmed by the massive change this would bring to us all. But Belinda and I both soon became confident of what God wanted us to do. *This is it!*

We accepted the position, but requested time to complete our major building project before telling the congregation, our friends, and our family. I did tell my parents, but no one else!

Our family was about to take a giant step, but God had prepared us for twelve years for this moment. We had seen, time after time, that if we were obedient, He was always faithful. Through faith, we had seen the impossible take place over and over again at the hand of the Lord.

The Scriptures say, "Faithful is He who calls you, and He also will do it" (1 Thessalonians 5:24, NASB). For our family, this next step was monumental. But we knew that He had called us, and we knew that He would do through us what He needed to do. We knew, *This is it!*

Is there a step God is calling you to take? Maybe He is

asking you to change jobs, start a new ministry, or move to a new city. Will you trust Him and obey His call?

Maybe, for you, *this is it!*

17

I DO NOT CARE IF AFRICA FALLS OFF THE FACE OF THE EARTH

After the building project was completed at Boynton UMC, I had plans to resign from the church and move my family to Africa.

Before the transition took place, I was asked to visit three countries in Africa to share the vision of Evangelism Explosion. One of those countries was Kenya, where they speak English. The other two were Zaire and Gabon, where they speak French. I do not speak French.

While I was in Kenya, I was to visit the mission school our children would attend, so I was looking forward to making the trip. But prior to leaving, I received a call. "Can you make the trip by yourself?" they asked. The executive vice president who had planned to make the journey with me was no longer able to go.

I'd never been to Africa before, but I said, "Sure, I can do that."

I was given an itinerary with people to meet, places to

stay, and where to be on various days. I was ready to go! I viewed the trip as an adventure. But I could have never guessed what was in store for me ahead.

My flight out was quite lengthy. I flew from Chattanooga to Atlanta, from Atlanta to Brussels, and from Brussels to Nairobi, Kenya—which is on the east coast of Africa. By the time I arrived, it had taken twenty-two hours. I was exhausted.

Thankfully, a missionary met me at the airport and took me to my room at a guest house. It was midnight there, and I was *more* than ready for bed. Just as I was falling asleep, I heard a noise rustle outside the window I had opened for some fresh air. *It could be a thief!* I thought. I had no idea—I'd never been to Africa before!

As it turned out, the noise I heard had been the property guard walking around. But it wasn't long before I was awake again. Leaving the window open had been a bad decision—there were mosquitos everywhere! Possibly carrying malaria! I decided to try and find another place to stay the next day.

Morning came and the same missionary who had met me the night before drove me to a church. There, I met with a number of missionaries and pastors to give my presentation of Evangelism Explosion's vision. The meeting went well! Next, I decided to find a map and drive myself to Rosslyn Academy, the school my children would attend. I picked up a map, rented a car, and was on my way.

Needless to say, driving in Kenya was *not* the same as driving in America. The steering wheel was on the right-hand side of the car, and I had to drive on the left side of the road, navigating roundabouts in heavy traffic. I had to drive very aggressively! Eventually, I found the school, but I was sweating by the time I got there!

When I went looking for a different place to stay, it was another arduous process. I went downtown and looked for something that would be a little closer to normal American accommodations. The first place I went into was no better than what I already had, so I decided to look at the Intercontinental Hotel. It looked and felt more familiar to me, and I was happy to find that they had rooms available.

After moving all of my things into my new hotel room, I decided to go into town and find some lunch. I was missing the comforts of home, so I ordered a burger with fries. Imagine my surprise when I bit into my burger, expecting it to taste like, well, a burger, and it was *nothing* like what I expected. *That's okay,* I thought. *At least I have my fries.* I went to pour a little ketchup sauce for dipping, and the entire lid fell off the bottle, soaking my entire plate! My server must have felt bad for me, because he came over to help.

As the days went by, I felt worse and worse. I was certain that I had a sinus infection. But there was no time to slow down because it was time for another flight, this time from Nairobi to Mombasa, a coastal city on the Indian Ocean.

Once in Mombasa, the missionary who was supposed to pick me up at the airport was nowhere to be found. The itinerary did not have a phone number or address listed for where I was supposed to go next. But the biggest obstacle was that in this part of Kenya, they spoke Swahili.

I remembered that the missionary who was supposed to meet me worked for an organization called Baptist Mission. So I found a taxi and asked if he could take me to First

Baptist Church. For some reason, the taxi driver also picked up a police officer and let him ride with us. After about half an hour, the police officer exited and we continued to the First Baptist Church in Mombasa.

Once there, I lugged my suitcase inside and talked to the pastor. He explained he had received English training from our ministry, so we were able to communicate. I asked if he could contact the Baptist missionary who was supposed to pick me up. He was able to make contact, so before long, the man arrived and drove me to his house. I was to stay there for the next two days.

The meetings in Mombasa went well, and then it was back to the Intercontinental Hotel in Nairobi. While staying there, I looked at some of the pamphlets in the bedside table and read that they also had a hotel located in Libreville, Gabon. I didn't realize it at the time, but this was very important information!

The following day I flew into Zaire. Someone met me at the airport, which I would come to be very thankful for. On our drive to the school for evangelism, he asked me where I was staying. I told him what was listed on my itinerary.

"No," he responded. "That's not a safe place. You will stay with us instead."

"Okay," I said. "I will call the hotel and cancel my reservation."

He pointed to a telephone and said, "The lines are down. It will not work."

What have I gotten myself into? I thought.

The meeting at the school went well but my sinus infection was getting worse. There was no medication to take so I was on my own. Either way, it was time for another flight.

The Zaire airport was in a situation of complete chaos. No one spoke English and there were no lines. Just people pushing and shoving to get to the counter. This was the first time I regretted making the trip alone. Finally, I was able to check in for my flight.

Just when I was ready to relax, several airport personnel approached me and walked me to a private room. My first thought was, *I'm never going to see my family again!* They were speaking French, and I had no idea what they wanted from me. They had me sit in a chair and began questioning me. I couldn't understand them and vice versa. They took my passport, which really made me nervous. *How will I ever get out of this country now?*

Praying, I said, "Lord, You say that You will never leave me nor forsake me. I believe You have a plan and purpose for me."

I could tell they wanted me to give them money. Their gesturing went on for what felt like an eternity, but it was probably only 10 to 15 minutes. Then they left me in the room for a while before returning. *Are they about to arrest me? This is serious!*

When they came back, they handed me my passport and let me go. I left the room, found my gate, and waited for my flight. *What was that?* I wondered, a bit shell-shocked. *I guess that's what it means to be fully dependent on the Lord!*

I arrived in my last country to visit, Gabon—another French-speaking nation. Once again, no one had come to the airport to pick me up. When I tried to make a phone call to the number listed on my itinerary, I realized the airport's phones were not working. I prayed and thought, *What am I going to do?*

Then I remembered—I was in *Libreville,* Gabon. I had read that there was an Intercontinental Hotel here. *Yes,* I thought, *that's where I'll stay. But I have to get there first.* I may not have had the local currency, but I did have some US dollars. I found a taxi driver and hoped he understood my request to take me to the hotel. Once again, a policeman got in the taxi and rode with us for about 20 minutes before exiting.

We arrived at the Intercontinental and I went inside. I basically guessed at what the French registration sheet was requesting, and was relieved when I was finally given a room. I paid the taxi driver and got on the elevator. *Finally,* I thought, *I may survive after all!*

Feeling exhausted and sick, I decided to call Belinda. It was Sunday morning there, and she was getting the kids ready for church—the same church who had no idea their pastor was about to resign and move to Africa. Only, I had decided that we weren't!

"I don't care if Africa falls off the face of the earth," I told Belinda. "We are *not* moving here!"

Belinda was shocked. Later, she told me she thought someone must have been holding a gun to my head. She knew it was unlike me to make such a statement.

Later that afternoon, I was able to get in touch with the missionary that was supposed to meet me. "We thought your flight was arriving tomorrow," he explained. He invited me to stay with him and his family, but I didn't have the energy to move!

"The hotel is fine," I told him.

That afternoon he picked me up, and I spoke to a group of pastors through a translator to explain our ministry. Everything seemed to go well, and for that, I was very thankful.

The following evening, I went back to the Libreville airport and got on a non-stop flight to Brussels. After about an hour of flying, the pilot announced that we were landing in Douala, Cameroon. We landed and taxied to the gate. It was nighttime there, but we were all asked to deplane. We then learned that there was a problem with the engine.

A balding man in a white T-shirt came along carrying a small toolbox. He walked to the engine while someone drove a car up to shine the high beams on the engine for lighting. The mechanic opened the cowling and looked inside. I'm not sure what he did, but he went to the other side of the engine next. After about 20 or 30 minutes, the mechanic was finished.

The pilots, without the passengers, taxied out a distance from the airport to perform an engine run-up test. Finally, they came back to the gate and allowed us back on the plane. We flew six hours over North Africa, the Mediterranean Sea, Europe, and then to Brussels. The flight from Brussels to Atlanta was straightforward and easy—no problems.

But on the short flight from Atlanta to Chattanooga, we experienced major turbulence. The plane lost altitude quickly, and everyone screamed. My dad was an Eastern

Airlines captain. Our family has traveled to many places in Europe and all across the United States. Never have I ever experienced such a drastic loss in altitude.

I thought, *I survived a severe sinus infection without medicine, I flew alone into three different African nations, I experienced an emergency landing in Cameroon—now I'm going to die on US soil?*

Thank God, that's not what happened. After we landed, I was beyond thankful to see Belinda at the Chattanooga airport. When we got home, I quickly unpacked my suitcase and gave my family the gifts I had picked up for them. One gift was a set of four wooden elephant napkin holders. Belinda placed them on our kitchen table, but when I looked at them, something strange happened. I was filled with a feeling I didn't quite understand.

"Put them away," I told her. "I don't want to see them."

Belinda knew that there was something wrong with me —something more than just the sinus infection. She sensed I was under spiritual attack. Later, she would share with me how she'd dropped to her knees after my phone call to her from Libreville. She'd prayed fervently, and the Lord had shown her that we *were* to move to Africa.

Despite Belinda's knowledge of the Lord's will, she allowed me space to work through my feelings. We didn't talk much more about it.

Several weeks passed and I made a call to my mother. The topic of Africa came up.

"Have you forgiven the person who was supposed to travel with you, but canceled?" she asked.

I hadn't.

"Have you forgiven the person who set up your itinerary?"

I hadn't.

"Have you forgiven the people who were supposed to meet you at airports, but didn't?"

Finally, I responded. "I haven't even thought about it. I didn't think I was upset with them."

We got off the phone and I began thinking about what my mother had asked me. I thought, *I'm not holding resentment against those people.* But after a few moments, it dawned on me —*I actually was!*

I immediately prayed, forgiving each person who played a role in the chaos of my trip. Then, I asked God to forgive me for my bad attitude. When I said, "I don't care if Africa falls off the face of the earth!" I had lost God's vision. But after forgiving others and asking for forgiveness, that vision was restored.

Twelve years prior, I had prayed, "Lord, I will be anything You want me to be. I will go anywhere You want me to go. I will do anything You want me to do."

God had clearly responded to me saying, "I am going to use you to reach hundreds of thousands of people for Me!" But after going there, I had allowed the events of the trip to block the vision the Lord had for me, for Belinda, and for our children.

Forgiveness is a powerful act. It can restore us to God, to ourselves, and to the vision the Lord has for our lives. Are you willing to pray and ask God, "Is there anyone I need to forgive or ask for their forgiveness? Is there anything in my life, Lord, that I need to ask You to forgive?"

1 John 1:8-9 (NASB) says, "If we say that we have no sin, we are deceiving ourselves and the truth is not in us. If we confess our sins, He is faithful and righteous, so that He will forgive us our sins and cleanse us from all unrighteousness."

Do you feel the Lord has given you a vision for your life that isn't coming to fruition? Maybe forgiveness is the key to unlocking the vision, releasing the full power of God into your life! Don't hesitate. Don't delay. If you need to forgive anyone, do it right now.

18

ARE YOU SURE YOU WANT ME TO DO THIS?

The day came for me to meet with my district superintendent and the bishop. It was time to discuss the topic of me leaving the pastorate and moving my family to Africa. I also had to ask them to assign me to EE International.

The morning before the meeting, I studied God's Word and prayed diligently. "Lord, I want to be sure that this is really what You want me to do. And that You will be with me wherever I go."

I still had questions. *What does this mean for our family?*

There was no guaranteed salary from a church, which is something we had gotten used to over the previous ten years. For the new missionary position, we had to raise all of the funds ourselves. Funds for my salary, for the airline tickets to Africa for our family of four, for the rental house, furniture and appliances, for a car and insurance, for the mission school fees for Timothy and Ann Marie, and for all other expenses.

Though I believed this was the direction our family should go, I was asking for just one more confirmation before the meeting. There were two things I needed to know: "Lord, I want to be sure this is really what You want me to do, and that You will be with me wherever I go."

As I was reading through the Bible, looking for answers to my two questions, I felt led to turn to the book of Joshua. This new direction was an extremely challenging task, not only for our family, but in terms of the ministry itself.

I came upon Joshua 1:6-7 and began reading. "Be strong and courageous, for you shall give this people possession of the land which I swore to their fathers to give them. Only be strong and very courageous; be careful to do according to all the law which Moses my servant commanded you. Do not turn from it to the right or to the left, so that you may have success wherever you go" (NASB).

That is it! I will have success wherever I go! Once again, the Lord had confirmed He wanted me to take the new position and move my family to Africa!

That was one question answered. I read on to verse 8, looking for the answer to the second question.

"This book of the Law shall not depart from your mouth, but you shall meditate on it day and night so that you may be careful to do according to all that is written in it; for then you will make your way prosperous, and then you will achieve success."

Yes! More confirmation. I kept reading.

"Have I not commanded you? Be strong and

courageous! Do not tremble or be dismayed, for the Lord your God is with you wherever you go" (v. 9).

The second question was, "Will You be with me wherever I go?"

God had answered!

I thanked God, closed my Bible, and got in my car to drive to Dalton, Georgia, to meet the superintendent and bishop.

I boldly shared my plans with them, not knowing how they would respond. The bishop looked at me and said, "Ron, instead of going to Africa, if you will stay, in your next appointment, I will assign you to one of the larger churches in the Atlanta area."

I thanked him, but said, "I believe this new direction is what I am supposed to do." After all, the Lord had just confirmed it!

The bishop added, "If you leave and later return to the pastorate, I cannot assure you the same appointment I am offering you today."

I said, "I understand." Inside, I thought, *I have burned the bridge. No time to look back now!*

The words from the book of Joshua continued to run through my mind. "Be strong and courageous . . . I will be with you wherever you go . . . I will give you success in whatever you do."

I remembered my prayer to the Lord, now almost 13 years prior. "I will be whatever You want me to be. I will go wherever You want me to go. I will do whatever You want me to do!"

Our family kept that promise I had made to the Lord. In

August of 1988, we moved to Africa! You'll have to keep reading to find out what happened next. But first, let's talk about you.

Where is God calling you? To Africa? To a different church body? To another state, job, or relationship?

You can be confident that wherever He has called you to, He will meet you there. He will go where you go and bring you success.

If you believe God has called you somewhere, do you need to pray and ask for confirmation? Pray and study God's Word. Listen. He will speak to you just as He did to me!

19

NO PLACE TO LIVE

The first order of business in preparing to leave for my new job with Evangelism Explosion (EE) was finding a place to live. We were moving from Ringgold, Georgia, to Nairobi, Kenya, located on the eastern coast of Africa. We had plans to stay in Atlanta with my parents in June and July of 1988 before departing for Africa in August. Only, we had no place to live once we got there. And no prospects.

Belinda and I both prayed earnestly for God to provide us with a place to live in Nairobi. We had to ship our belongings by container, and they would not be arriving in Mombasa until late October, so we needed somewhere furnished to stay from August through October. Though we had no idea where we'd lay our heads in just a few short weeks, we had faith God would provide.

On our last weekend in Ringgold, Belinda and I took the kids to the ballpark to watch Timothy's baseball game. Sitting in the stands, Belinda noticed a little boy running around. He was wearing a shirt that said, "I love Kenya." She kept watching the small boy until finally, she stood up and approached him.

"Is your mom here?" Belinda asked.

"Sure!" The little boy took Belinda to where his mom was sitting.

"Can you tell me where you got your son's shirt?" Belinda asked.

"From the Warren family," the boy's mom explained. "They are close friends of ours, and they're missionaries in Nairobi, Kenya."

Before you get excited, let me just tell you—the story gets *even better*!

Belinda spent a few more minutes speaking with the mom, who said, "The Warrens are in the US now, actually. They are staying with a family just a few miles from here. I can give you a number to reach them."

When we got home that afternoon, we gave them a call and asked if we might stop in to speak with them. They happily agreed!

We were pleased to learn we had a good deal in common with the Warrens. The president of EE was the same denomination as the Warren's mission organization. They were quite familiar with EE too. What were the chances?

So we asked our burning question: "Do you have any suggestions for where we might live in Nairobi from August through the end of October?"

"Actually," they said, "we do."

They explained that their fundraising had been a bit

short. Although they were originally supposed to return to Nairobi in August, they now had to stay in the United States for a few more months so that they could raise the needed support. Mr. Warren concluded, "If you would like, you are welcome to rent our Nairobi house. It is totally furnished with a kitchen, three bedrooms, and a living room. Our local help there will take care of everything for you—you do not even need to hire anyone. Everything is already in place for you."

And that's exactly what we did.

In a matter of hours, we went from having no place to live to having a *perfect* place to live. It was amazing! If we had not been in Ringgold, Georgia and not at Timothy's game . . . had Belinda not noticed the little boy running around . . . if his mother had not dressed him in that shirt that day! It's incredible how God can orchestrate complex solutions in the simplest of ways.

What solution are you waiting on God to orchestrate? What do you stand in need of today? Like He did with us, God is waiting on you to be attentive to His plan for you.

Are you ready to allow God to supply your needs? Are you prepared to pray, and then place the weight of your request in His hands?

God will surely be faithful to supply your needs according to His riches in glory in Christ Jesus.

20

DO NOT COME

We had said all of our goodbyes. We'd said goodbye to our church family and our friends. We'd driven to Madison, Georgia, to say goodbye to Belinda's parents, her sister, and other family members. Then we'd come back to Atlanta to where my parents lived to stay our last few days in the US.

Everything was set and ready to go. We had shipped our container holding almost all of our earthly possessions to the New Orleans area, where it would eventually be picked up and sent to Kenya. Our children were registered at Rosslyn Academy in Nairobi. We had our rental home lined up. And we'd purchased four airline tickets that would take us and our two kids around the world from Atlanta to Brussels, and then from Brussels to Nairobi.

There was only one thing missing, and it was important: our work permits. In order for any American to perform Christian ministry work in the country of Kenya, they were required to apply for and obtain a work permit. Belinda and

I applied twice and were denied both times. The field director in Kenya sent us a message with the news of the second denial, and concluded by saying, "Do not come."

We weren't certain why we had been denied, but we continued to have faith that God was at work. In fact, Belinda and I were so certain of our calling to go to Kenya with EE, that we were almost *excited* to see just how God was going to work it all out.

What made the situation even more interesting was the fact that after your second denial for a work permit, there was a waiting period before you could apply again. We did not have time to reapply—our flight was scheduled for the very next Friday!

God had a lot of work to do in just a few days' time, but we had seen Him do the impossible for us over and over again. We were confident this roadblock would be no different. Thirteen years prior, He'd spoken a promise into my life, and God would no doubt see it come to pass.

It was our last Sunday in Atlanta and I was scheduled to speak at all three morning services at First United Methodist Church in Marietta, Georgia. The senior pastor of the church, Reverend Charles Sineath, had planned for Belinda and me to be commissioned during the services as well. To be commissioned is the process of blessing someone and affirming the use of the gifts God has given them. Usually, it involves a corporate prayer over a person, couple, or group before they leave to start a new ministry.

My message that Sunday was about praising and thanking God in all things and for all things. I taught that we should believe God can and will take impossible situations and accomplish them on our behalf. I told God that morning, "I can't wait to see how You are going to solve our work permit problem! I know that nothing is impossible with You!"

We hadn't shared with the congregation that our work permits had been denied. During the second worship service, I leaned over to Pastor Sineath and told him what our family was facing. "The field director has said to us, 'Do not come.'"

He began laughing quietly. He said, "Ron, now I *know* you are going to Kenya!"

Throughout the previous week, we not only prayed for God's provision for us, we thanked Him in advance for it. We praised Him. We told the Lord, "We look forward to seeing how You will accomplish that which seems to us to be impossible."

The following day was Monday. Our last Monday in Atlanta—only five days before we were supposed to board a plane for Africa. The telephone rang at my parents' house. My father said, "Ron! The phone is for you!"

I picked up the telephone. "Hello?"

It was the field director from Kenya. "Ron," he said, "I don't understand how this happened, but yours and Belinda's work permits are sitting on my desk. You can come to Kenya!"

We hadn't even been able to apply a third time! And the work permits just *appeared*. This was truly a miracle!

What do you do when you are faced with a situation that appears to be a giant roadblock? What do you believe to be true about God when you're faced with a situation that seems impossible? Do you walk around disappointed? Discouraged? Or dismayed?

The lyrics of the song, "Turn Your Eyes Upon Jesus" go:

> *Turn your eyes upon Jesus,*
> *Look full into His wonderful face,*
> *And the things of earth will grow strangely dim,*
> *In the light of His glory and grace.*"[1]

When the clock is ticking down on a deadline and you're waiting on the Lord to intervene, simply turn your eyes upon Jesus. Look to Him. Worship Him. Praise Him. Thank Him in advance for doing what only He can do—the impossible.

In Philippians 4:19 it says, "My God shall supply all your needs according to His riches in glory in Christ Jesus." This is a verse that has been a theme in my family's ministry and life. But the same is true for you.

God called us to go. He knew our need. And He supplied exactly what was needed for us to answer His call.

Philippians 4:4 says, "Rejoice in the Lord always, again I will say, Rejoice!" You, too, can rejoice in the Lord always. Regardless of what your circumstances are, you have a choice in how you'll respond. Will you rejoice? Will you thank God for doing the impossible before He's done it?

"Do not come," they had told us.

But God had the last word. He will have the last word in your situation too. In the meantime, rejoice!

21

WILL THE LORD TAKE CARE OF OUR FAMILY?

We landed in the mile-high city of Nairobi, Kenya, on a cold, rainy day. We hadn't been expecting that type of weather. Belinda rummaged around in one of our carry-on bags, looking for sweaters to put on Timothy, now nine, and Ann Marie, now eight.

"My tummy still feels funny," complained Ann Marie. She had air sickness for most of the flight, and she was still nauseated. We were tired, damp, chilly, and hungry.

Later, Timothy walked up to Belinda and handed her something. She looked and then showed it to me. It was a filling that had randomly fallen out of his tooth!

"Do they have dentists in Nairobi?" Belinda asked. I didn't know.

It wasn't the arrival I had anticipated, but Belinda and I were confident we were right where God wanted us. I also kept in mind the promise the Lord had made to me over a decade before—that He would use me to reach thousands. I knew being Vice President of Evangelism Explosion and introducing, developing, and overseeing our ministry in Africa was God's answer to that promise.

Besides, who else could have orchestrated a former schoolteacher and former programmer/analyst to quit their jobs, enter full-time ministry, then uproot their family and take them to Africa? Only God. He surely wouldn't desert us now.

But even with all God had already done, in that moment, with the kids cold, Ann Marie sick, Timothy's sudden dental need, and all of us standing in the rain, I wondered, *What are we doing here?*

Neither Belinda nor I spoke it out loud, but at the time, we were both thinking, *If only we could have stayed on that plane and gone back to America!*

Belinda had been praying earnestly, *Lord, I need to know that you will take care of our family. Will you take care of all our needs?*

We made our way through security and customs and met a car outside the airport. We loaded up our luggage, hoping we had everything we would need during the three months we'd be spending without our container. Then we set off for the mission guest house where we were staying for a few days.

That first night we sat down for dinner at a table of missionaries. It struck me in that moment: *Wait. Now we're missionaries too!* The house we were at was sort of a stop-over for missionaries in the area who lived "up-country." They would drive to Nairobi, buy the supplies they needed, stay the night, then drive back to their stations of ministry.

Belinda began a conversation with one of the men at the table. You'll never guess what this man's profession was. Just try! He was a *dentist* back in the US, and he was stationed just an hour away from us in Kenya. He would only be at the guest house for one night—the exact night we arrived!

Dr. Rich, the dentist, asked to see Timothy's mouth. "I can fix this right up! Can you drive out to my mission station?"

We readily agreed. A few days later we borrowed a car and drove to the Rift Valley mission station.

The office was one room with two dentist chairs for patients. In one chair, a Kenyan man was seated. A female dentist had her hands in his mouth, working on the man. It appeared that she was trying to pull one of the man's teeth out, but was having trouble. Belinda and I gave each other a look, thinking the same thing: *She looks like she's struggling to pull out that tooth!*

Dr. Rich had Timothy in the other chair, and we were standing beside them. On the other side of the room, the female dentist stood up on her chair, trying to get enough leverage to pull out the man's tooth. All of us just stared, unsure of what to do. It reminded me of a scene in a movie, *The Shakiest Gun in the West*, with the actor Don Knotts who played the part of a dentist.

I looked down at Timothy, who had an indescribable look on his face. Dr. Rich got up to help. Timothy watched intently, as did the rest of us. What would he do? With a flick of his wrist and a little maneuvering, Dr. Rich was able to extract the man's tooth. He returned to Timothy, leaving the other dentist to finish the procedure.

"Ready?" he asked our son. I'm sure Belinda was ready —ready to yank Timothy up and run to the airport to take him to an American dental office. But she remained calm.

Dr. Rich was able to fill Timothy's tooth with no problems. When he was finished, Dr. Rich asked Timothy how he felt.

"That was easy!" he replied. "It didn't hurt at all."

Belinda prayed, "Lord, will you take care of our family?" And within the first few days of being in Kenya, God showed us that He would.

Are you standing in the rain somewhere, wondering, *What am I doing here?* Do you believe that the Lord has a purpose for you there? Ask Him to reveal that purpose, or to remind you of it.

Ask Him to provide whatever you are in need of right now. And then, watch His faithfulness as he takes care of you and your family!

22

HOW DO YOU WANT ME TO DO THIS?

The week before our family flew from Atlanta to Nairobi, I called Dr. James Kennedy, the president and founder of Evangelism Explosion.

"Any last words for me before our family moves to Kenya?"

"Bring Evangelism Explosion into every nation of Africa," he charged.

It had been two months since he'd spoken those words to me. Our shipping container had arrived, and we were living in our rental home. The home was perfect for us, with a detached garage that I planned to use as an office. In that office, I had a small desk and a chair. I also had a map of Africa taped to the wall.

I looked at that map and began writing in a notebook that I kept on my desk next to my Bible. I wrote down the name of every nation, along with the language spoken there. Fifty-three countries—that was a lot. Later, I would come to realize that Africa represents ¼ of the world's nations.

"Lord," I prayed, "How do you want me to do this? How can I bring EE and the gospel message into every one of these countries? Where do you want me to start?"

As I prayed, I was reminded of several Scriptures from the Bible. Luke 1:37, "For nothing is impossible with God" (NASB). And Philippians 4:13, "I can do all things through Christ who strengthens me" (NKJV). And then, Joshua 1:9, "Have I not commanded you? Be strong and courageous! Be not terrified nor dismayed, for the LORD your God is with you wherever you go" (NASB). I also recalled Psalm 46:10 (NASB), "Stop *striving* and know that I am God . . ."

More Scriptures came to mind. 1 Thessalonians 5:16-18. Proverbs 3:5-7. The Lord was directing me step-by-step, one verse at a time. He was saying, "Follow me. I will lead you."

I prayed, "Thank You, Lord. I can't wait to see what You are going to do next."

Later on, people would ask me, "What was your master plan?"

I responded, "I did not have one. I just listened to the Master's plan through prayer. He revealed His plan to me as needed, and I simply obeyed."

As I was thinking through what strategy to use to get started, I remembered how airlines have "hubs" in certain cities. God spoke, "Create hubs in Africa."

So that's where I started. Initially, I created a hub in East Africa, which is where Nairobi is. Next, I created a Southern African hub that was located in Pretoria. I established an

English-speaking hub in West Africa, and a French-speaking hub in West Africa. I also placed a hub in Central Africa. Lastly, I established a hub in North Africa.

As I prayed, I believed that with God, *nothing* would be impossible.

Next, I asked the Lord to help me find people to receive the training for our ministry. God opened up doors for me to meet people to work in these different hubs. After selecting each person, I would fly them to a location where they spoke the language—French, English, or Arabic. One-by-one, each hub was staffed.

Prayer is essential in planning. I prayed before receiving direction. I prayed at the time of receiving direction. And I prayed after receiving direction, as I carried out His plan.

I cannot overemphasize the importance of prayer. James 5:16 tells us that the prayers of a righteous man (that includes women, teenagers, and children) are powerful and effective. Through prayer—combined with the disciplines of rejoicing always and giving thanks in the midst of challenging circumstances—I saw God accomplish the impossible.

When we moved to Africa in August of 1988, five African nations had started the Evangelism Explosion ministry. By December 28, 1995, in just seven years, the EE ministry was in every last nation of Africa—all 53 of them, with Libya being the last.

It only took seven (the Lord's perfect number of completion) years for God to help me fulfill my mission to bring EE to the entire continent. I had prayed, "God, I can't wait to see how this will be done!" Step-by-step, decision-by-decision, country-by-country, He'd led me through it.

What situation are you facing right now that you need God to lead you through? What's your plan? Have you asked God to guide your every move? Are you willing to "be still" and "stop striving" to allow God to be God?

Walk with the Master, who will give you His plan—the Master's plan!

23

WHY DID YOU WAIT SO LONG TO COME?

In training people on how to share their faith with their villages and churches, I did something called "OJT," or on-the-job training. I believed it wasn't enough to simply give them information, but for them to apply the training in real-life scenarios. The goal was for them to be able to evangelize on their own, and for them to be able to train their church members to do the same.

So we'd go out into the local areas and share the gospel. During one such outing, I was doing OJT with one American and two Nigerian pastors. We walked out into a village where we were approached by a bunch of children. The children were talking to us and clamoring for our attention. The Nigerian pastor translated their words to me, but I had a feeling that God wanted us to continue walking.

As we walked deeper into the village, we encountered five elderly men sitting on a wall. One of the men said something to me that I didn't understand.

"What did he say?" I asked the translator.

"He said, 'Come and tell us about God.'"

That, I thought, *I can do!*

Through the translator, I spoke to the men, hoping to establish some sort of relationship.

Eventually, I asked, "Have you come to the place in your life where you know for certain that if you were to die today, you would go to Heaven?"

"No," was the response from all five men.

Then I said, "May I share with you how I know for certain that I have eternal life?"

Each man said, "Yes."

I went on to say, "Before I do, may I ask each of you a second question?"

Again, the men said, "Yes."

"If you were to die today and stand before God, and He were to ask you, 'Why should I let you into Heaven?', what would you say to God?"

Each man answered that question. "God would not let me into His Heaven."

Then I said, "When I heard each of your answers to the first question, I thought I might have some good news to share with you. But now, after hearing your answers to the second question, I know I have *the best news* anyone could ever hear!"

Then I presented the gospel. When I was finished, I asked, "Does that make sense to you?"

"Yes!" came their resounding responses.

"Would you like to receive the gift of eternal life?"

I waited for each man to answer, one by one. "This is an

important decision," I added. "So first, let me clarify what you are about to do."

The American trainee with us was getting anxious. He wanted the men to pray the prayer of salvation right away.

"There's no reason to rush," I told him. "We are going to take the time for each man to understand the decision he is going to make. Besides, there are no satellite dishes installed in this village. They aren't going anywhere! There are no distractions here."

I explained the steps of salvation once again. Once I was certain each man understood what they were about to do, they confirmed, "Yes, I want to pray to receive Christ!"

After their prayer, we congratulated the men. "Welcome to the family of God!"

Before leaving, one of the men stopped to ask me, "Did your father know about Jesus?"

"Yes," I said.

"How long have you known about this Jesus?" he asked.

I thought for a moment and then gave him my answer.

The man looked a bit confused. "Then why did you wait so long to come?" he asked.

Even today that question rings through my mind!

"I can't answer that question," I told him, "but I can tell you that we're here to stay. Though I won't be living in this area, in this village, these two men right here will!" I pointed toward the two Nigerian pastors.

Our team of four walked back to the church where we were conducting the training. Once there, I asked the two Nigerian pastors to report what had just happened.

We continued the training the next day. To our surprise,

the five men from the wall came to the church as we were finishing up.

"Can we tell everyone what happened yesterday?" they asked.

"Yes!" I exclaimed.

The five men stood before the pastors being trained and shared their story of salvation. Then, they asked if they could stay for the remainder of our training to learn more.

"Of course!" we all answered. "You are welcome."

"Why did you wait so long to come?" the man had asked me. Maybe God is asking you that same question. What is He calling you toward or asking you to do? Are you tarrying, dragging your feet, or complaining?

Are you willing to look at the Lord and say, "I am ready. I'll go where You send me!"?

People are waiting to hear a word from God—people like the five men on the wall. Will you go? Will you tell them about Jesus? They are waiting!

24

DOES THIS MEAN AIRPLANE
EXPLOSION?

One time, I flew into the nation of Zimbabwe, formerly known as Rhodesia. During this trip, I met with our leadership team and spoke at several events. When I was finished with my tasks, it was time to fly to my next destination, departing from the Bulawayo airport.

The leadership of the EE ministry in Zimbabwe had created the "Teacher Training Board" to be used for training pastors. The dimensions of the board were quite large, with a hole at the top the size of a quarter. The board was painted black on both sides. The material of the back side was created to be used as a chalkboard by the teacher

On the front side was a printed diagram that we called the "Visual Advance Organizer." Simple pictures had been drawn inside a diamond-shaped outline. Nothing unique, but helpful in training pastors in remote areas of the country.

The teacher placed the board on a tree by hanging it on

a nail. It helped the students to see the board. The drawings and pictures were easily discernable, colored in gold. The pictures helped the teacher explain how their trainees should present the gospel. Across the top of the board was printed in large, capital letters: "EVANGELISM EXPLOSION."

At our Zimbabwe office, I picked up one of these boards. Instead of checking it with my suitcase, I brought it onto the plane with my carry-on luggage to make sure it was not damaged.

Over the loudspeaker, my flight number and destination were announced. It was time to board! My boarding pass was checked with no problem. The next step, however, was different. I walked up to the security platform and laid down my suitcase along with the training board.

The security agent picked up the board and turned it over to the front. He held it up for all to see. Then he pointed to "EVANGELISM EXPLOSION" and asked me in a stern voice, "Does this mean 'Airplane Explosion?'"

In today's terrorism climate, especially at airports, it was not the time to make a joke with security!

I said, "Evangelism Explosion is not destruction, but multiplication."

He seemed to consider my response.

I went on, "In the last few years, the world has experienced a 'population explosion.' We want to encourage an 'evangelism explosion' to all those people around the entire world. We want everyone to know about Jesus."

The security agent seemed interested in hearing more. So I said, "'Multiplication,' is many people moving from unbelief to belief in Jesus Christ. Instead of addition, we want to multiply."

Eventually, I boarded the plane and made it to my next destination. I felt much better after experiencing the security agent's response to my explanation. Though I had not led him in the sinner's prayer, I had planted a seed. I prayed he would one day come to know Jesus personally, and that he too would experience the "multiplication" we were so passionate about.

Do your friends, neighbors, and co-workers know that you are a Christian? Can they tell by your words and actions? When people know that you are a Christian, they are looking to you for answers. What will your answers be?

You may never get asked if you're carrying around a board about an "Airplane Explosion," but if you follow Christ, you may be questioned at some point regarding what you believe. Are you ready to give an answer? Not knowing what the other person may ask next?

You may never be in a Muslim country when the security agent opens your carry-on luggage, discovers a Bible, and asks, "Is this your Bible?" But what would you say to your co-worker who may see you bless your food before you eat it? What will you say to your neighbor who asks, "What do you believe?"

Always be prepared to give an answer for your faith.

25

I CANNOT WAIT TO SEE HOW YOU WILL ACCOMPLISH THIS

I was in bad shape. Not only did I have a severe sinus infection, but I had torn my left calf muscle, so I was wearing a cast on my leg and using crutches to get around.

Periodically throughout the day, I would hobble on my crutches from my office to our upstairs bedroom so that I could lie down and rest for a while. On this particular day, my heart was heavy. I was supposed to travel to Niger and Chad that year in order to bring the ministry of EE to their nations. I knew as I lay in bed, feeling miserable, that I would not be in any condition to board a plane and take the necessary steps to accomplish that goal.

I prayed, "God, You love the people of Chad and Niger more than I do. You created them. You know I am not able to fly. So I cannot wait to see how you will accomplish this."

As I was still praying, the telephone rang. That was a miracle in itself—the phones rarely worked! I picked up the phone and began speaking to the caller, whose name was Fraser. He and his wife were good friends of ours.

I said, "What are you doing right now?"

"I am planning a conference at Brackenhurst," he said. "I am bringing in leaders from around Africa."

Brackenhurst was about 45 minutes from my house. The wheels in my head started spinning. "Fraser, would you possibly have anyone in these meetings from Chad or Niger?"

"Absolutely," he said.

My excitement was growing. I love watching God's plans come together! I explained to Fraser my responsibilities to bring EE to Chad and Niger, and also my physical predicament.

"I am more than happy to help you," Fraser said. "Here's what we'll do. I will send a driver to your house to pick you up. You can lie down in the backseat and rest while you travel. I will set up meetings for you with leaders from Chad and Niger. The driver will wait for you until you are finished and then drive you back home."

I took Fraser up on his offer and met with the leaders. After explaining the EE ministry and our plans, I asked them to go back to their nations and select two pastors they would recommend to go through our training. "I will pay for these pastors' expenses, their flights, and their lodging while they receive our training. The selected pastors will return to their nation and train their members. Then, next year I will fly to them and help them train other pastors."

Wouldn't you know it—that's *exactly* what happened. We were able to add Chad and Niger to our list of African nations practicing the EE ministry. And I didn't even have to leave Kenya for it to happen!

I had prayed, "God, you know I'm not physically able to accomplish the task I've been given. But I know you will find a way to accomplish your will, with or without me!"

What are you facing today that only God can accomplish? Are you willing to pray, "God, do whatever You have to do in order for Your perfect will to be done!"? Do you believe that God can and will respond?

It may not happen the way you want it to, it may not happen the way *you* plan it, but God is a big God who can do anything we ask of Him according to His will.

26

ENOUGH JET FUEL TO REACH ABIDJAN

Upon completing some meetings in South Africa, my next destination was Ivory Coast, a French-speaking nation located in West Africa.

In Johannesburg, South Africa, I boarded a non-stop flight on the Air Afrique airline. Sitting in my seat, I waited for departure.

The flight time was about six hours, traveling across Africa then over the Atlantic Ocean before reaching land at Abidjan, a major city located in the nation of Ivory Coast.

As always, I prayed while the plane taxied out to the end of the runway. I asked God for a safe trip, that the flight crew would be healthy, and that the Lord would give wisdom to the pilots in dealing with any difficult weather or airplane problems. I also asked that it would be a comfortable flight for all of the passengers. This was a normal routine for me.

But as I was praying, a different thought came to my

mind. *Pray that we will have enough jet fuel to reach Abidjan.* Before that day, I had never prayed that request, and have never prayed it again. One may think that is a strange prayer. But I prayed it anyway!

Over many years, when a thought comes to my mind to pray, I just do it. I do not try to question why—I just pray! Scripture is filled with thoughts on prayer. One I remember often is to "pray without ceasing." To me that means throughout the day, I am acknowledging God's presence in my life. He is with me. This is very comforting. It is a way of life!

The plane took off from Johannesburg. The flight was smooth, with no problems. We landed in Abidjan on time.

I departed the airplane, went through security, picked up my luggage, went through customs, and walked into the lobby to meet my friend who normally met me at the airport. To my surprise, he was not there.

I thought, *That is strange. He is always on time.* I assumed he must be delayed due to traffic. I waited, and waited, and waited. He still had not arrived, so I decided to do some work on a project that needed my attention. After about an hour-and-a-half, my friend arrived at the airport.

I asked, "Why were you so late today?"

He explained, "Before coming to the airport, I called the airline and asked if your flight would be on time. They said no, that the plane was to make another stop at a different airport before arriving in Abidjan."

I asked my friend, "Did they say why the extra landing?"

"The extra landing was to refuel," he said. "So the flight was going to be late."

"May we have enough jet fuel to reach Abidjan," the Lord had prompted me to pray. I'm not sure why God didn't want us to stop in another airport before reaching Abidjan. Perhaps some calamity might have befallen us there. There are many things I'm certain the Lord has saved me from that I don't want to know the details of!

The Bible tells us to trust in the Lord with all our heart, and lean not on our own understanding. What might have happened if I had told the Lord, "No, I'm not going to pray for enough fuel. That's strange!"? I don't know, and I'm thankful I don't know.

Are you listening for that still, small voice when you pray? Are you only speaking the words *you* want to speak? Or do you allow God time to respond to you?

Prayer is meant to be a two-way conversation. Pause, listen, and be obedient to what He says back to you.

27

GOES ON AND ON

In sharing with people in Africa, I saw many coming to Christ. I also saw many people learning how to share their faith, and in turn, how to train others to do the same.

I thought, *We have our training materials translated and printed in several languages, but we cannot reach a large portion of the people in Africa—those who can barely read or write and those who are illiterate.*

I prayed, "What about those people? How do You want to reach them?"

God responded with this answer, "Use pictures!"

Well, we already had simple pictures. But because our materials were focused mostly on the words, we didn't reference the pictures and drawings very much.

While our family was in South Africa, we visited a gold mine which was no longer active. We rode an elevator down a long underground shaft. After the elevator stopped, we came out into a maze of underground tunnels. As we walked through one of the tunnels, I saw pictures on the walls. The tour guide explained that the mine workers did not all speak the same language. So they drew pictures to explain to the workers how to carry out their responsibilities.

A light went on in my mind. *This is it!* A confirmation of what the Lord had said to me: "Use pictures!" This was the way to reach the people who could barely read or write! The people who were illiterate!

Not long after that, I flew to the country of Zimbabwe. In Bulawayo, a major city, I met with our national director. We created a small booklet of pictures and a training notebook which we called the "FlipChart." The layout we designed could be printed on two pieces of A4 paper (the size of paper most commonly used in Africa), and then folded, cut, and stapled to create a nice booklet. The person being trained could look at each picture and remember the stories and Scriptures which had been explained to them.

The side of the paper facing the trainee was only one picture. The back side was a small copy of the picture and a simple written outline explaining the picture—this was for the trainer.

The national director selected Tsholotsho (pronounced cho-low-cho), a small village in Zimbabwe, to field test the training. Most of the people in Tsholotsho could not read or write.

Later that year I flew back to Zimbabwe. A few of us drove the long distance to Tsholotsho to find out how the training went. We interviewed the people who were trained.

In the interviews I asked them, "In what ways were the materials effective?"

We received very positive responses!

One lady described her specific experience. During the training, the lady would practice at home, giving the presentation to her ten-year-old daughter. The mother would look at each picture in the booklet, then give the gospel presentation from memory. While practicing, the daughter prayed to receive Jesus!

The daughter asked her mother if she would teach her how to do the training. Her mother did, and the daughter learned the gospel presentation too! Then, she would use what she had learned to present the gospel to her friends. Several of her friends in the village even prayed to receive Jesus!

The same lady told another story. One evening she was practicing, saying the gospel out loud, and her husband came into the house. He heard his wife and asked, "What are you doing?"

She told him that she was practicing how to tell someone how they could have eternal life, and how the person can know for certain they will go to Heaven someday.

Her husband was not a Christian. She looked at him and started talking to him about what she had learned. She presented the gospel to her husband, and her husband prayed to receive Jesus as his Lord and Savior.

Another lady gave me a gift she had made for my wife. It was a hand-made crochet lace doily. It had a beautiful center area surrounded by a circle, then a larger circle, then even larger circles moving to the outside of the doily. I did not realize, and did not think anyone else realized either, how appropriate the design was—something I would not discover until the end of the meeting.

Throughout the interview that day, several more people gave testimonies of how the FlipChart training had helped them. The pastor in the village said, "Other groups have come to our village and they talked to us about Jesus. That was good, but that was all. They never gave us a method to tell others about Jesus. What you have done is different. You have equipped us to be able to present the gospel to other people in this particular area of Zimbabwe."

In Africa, names have meaning. The village named "Tsholotsho" did as well. I asked, "What is the meaning of your village's name?"

One of the leaders said, "Goes on and on!"

I was amazed at the meaning, "Goes on and on!" I said. "Tell me again, what is the meaning of 'Tsholotsho'?"

Again the leader said, "Goes on and on!"

I was so excited! Why? Because the village of Tsholotsho was the first place the FlipChart had been tested in Africa. The first place anywhere in the world that the training had been tested.

I said, "Have you ever dropped a small stone in the middle of a puddle of water? What happens? It creates rings, a rippling effect, starting with the center, and moving out. It goes on and on!"

Tsholotsho was indeed just the beginning. The

FlipChart training was used in other parts of Africa, and then around the world! It goes on and on—starting in Tsholotsho and spreading throughout Zimbabwe, throughout other countries in Africa, and through other places around the world!

The people were excited. They understood. Their small village was the beginning, but it would not stop there. It would go on and on, "Tsholotsho!"

The village of Tsholotsho had been experiencing a drought. It had not rained for several months. Earlier in the meeting we had prayed for rain. What happened next? You guessed it! When we finished the meeting, it began to rain! The people did not look for umbrellas. They ran outside and began looking at the center of the puddles of water as the rain landed, creating rings and rings, further out from the center.

They began pointing down at each one of these areas where the rings had spread out, and saying, "Tsholotsho, Tsholotsho, Tsholotsho!" *It goes on and on. It goes on and on!*

The design of the crochet lace doily told their story as well. What started in their village was the pebble dropping into water. It would go on and on.

What about you? Has the gospel you once learned stopped with you? Or have you been like the people of Tsholotsho? Have you told others about Jesus with your life and words? Has the message of Jesus gone out from you?

It is an amazing privilege that every believer and follower of Jesus Christ gets to share of God's goodness with a daughter, a husband, a village, a community, and beyond.

Will you be the one to share the gospel with another person? Will you say, "I am ready to start the ripple effect!"?

If you do, know that your actions will affect more people than just you or the person you share with. Like the village of Tsholotsho, it will go on and on and on.

28

I HAVE NEVER SEEN ANYTHING
LIKE THIS

In the mid-1990s, the managing director of an African seminary asked me to come to his school and teach a class. (A managing director would be like the president of any US seminary.)

I said, "I will come and teach three sessions explaining how to share one's faith. But my requirement in accepting this invitation is that the last session will not be in the classroom, but the entire class will go to Nairobi Park to talk with people. I will supply trainers to lead the conversations. Each trainer will have two students, which will make up a team of three people."

I went on to explain that this would give students the opportunity to experience a live situation, and hopefully, to hear the gospel presented. More OTJ training!

The managing director was quite pleased with my requirements. He said, "Normally, the students just listen to teaching in the classroom, but are never in a live application setting." He went on, "I want to come with the students, and Ron, I want to be on your team."

We both agreed to the plan.

The day came for the students to go to the park. As we were driving there, the managing director said to me, "I set up two businessmen to meet us today in the park to hear the gospel."

I responded, "Okay." Then I parked my car, and we walked into the park, where we waited for the two businessmen.

In advance, all the teams had prayed that God would prepare the hearts of the people we would meet and share with that afternoon.

While we were waiting for the two businessmen to show up, another man walked up and started talking to us. I was not sure if I really wanted to talk to this man. I thought, *Does he want to sell us something, or does he really want to talk?*

Then I figured I would go ahead and present the gospel to him. If he wasn't interested, he could walk away. I started by asking him my normal questions: Have you come to a place in your life where you're confident that if you died today, you'd go to Heaven?

He said, "No."

I looked around, thinking the two businessmen would show up any second, but they did not.

So I continued, "May I ask you another question?" He agreed. So I said, "Suppose you were to die today and stand before God, and He were to ask you, 'Why should I let you into Heaven?', what would you say to God?'"

The man's response was, "There is nothing I have done. I do not deserve to be in Heaven."

I went on and presented the gospel. When I got to the end, I said, "Does this make sense to you?"

He responded, "Yes!"

Then I asked, "Would you like to receive the gift of eternal life?"

Again, he said, "Yes!"

I looked around and saw that the two businessmen still had not arrived.

So, I went through the clarification with this man to make sure he understood the decision he was making. Next, I led him in a prayer to receive Jesus as his Savior. We set up another time to meet so I could follow up with him about his decision.

The two businessmen never showed up that day.

As we walked back to my car, the managing director looked at me, overwhelmed with what he had just seen happen. "I have never seen anything like this before!" He was so pleased that he and his students experienced a real, live application of sharing their faith.

God continues to look for people who are willing to share a story about His faithfulness. Can you think of a story that you could tell? If you do not have your own story, think of a story you have been told. People love hearing stories!

If you are willing, ask God to send someone into your life that you can share your story with—someone you can share the gospel with.

No matter how many people I have led to Christ, it is

still miraculous and amazing to me every single time. I know God feels the same way!

29

MY FATHER SEES WHAT YOU ARE DOING

Belinda became very involved in several different ministries once we arrived in Nairobi.

Of course, she was also deeply committed to our children. We used to say that because I traveled so much, Belinda "held down the hut." We didn't actually live in a hut, but we did live in Africa.

Belinda is a kind, loving person, who is precious to me. She is a wonderful mother and wife! Belinda cares about other people. She has a gentle spirit, and a deep love for her Lord, Jesus Christ.

That's why it was no surprise to me that Belinda created several of her own ministries to run in Nairobi. One was a ministry with wives of husbands who worked in different nations' embassies that were located in Nairobi. She also led a Bible study out of our home. And she helped me with my Evangelism Explosion work. But perhaps one of Belinda's greatest contributions started in the streets.

In Nairobi, Kenya, you could always see beggars in the streets.

Uganda is a bordering nation to Kenya. Though there were Ugandan refugee women begging in the streets of Nairobi, a small group of them were different. Why were they different? Their husbands had been workers in the office of the President of Uganda. These men were killed in the war, leaving their wives and children behind. Their families fled to Kenya after their deaths.

These Ugandan refugee women were former teachers and secretaries. Now, you found them begging on the streets of Nairobi. They were in a foreign land. Their children were hungry and homeless.

Back when we were living in the US, getting ready to move to Africa, Belinda felt led to pack her cross-stitch materials and books. Several of the books were Precept Ministries materials written by Kay Arthur. One of Kay's books is *Lord, I Want to Know You*. That book teaches about the different names of God.

It had been several years since we had unpacked our container in Nairobi. Belinda saw the Ugandan refugee women. Like her, they were in a foreign land, but their children were hungry and homeless. As she saw these women, God gently nudged her to help.

"But how?" she asked God.

He then reminded Belinda of the cross-stitch materials she had packed, along with a book on the names of God—a name to meet every need! She immediately retrieved those items and got to work.

Belinda, along with another missionary, taught these

ladies how to cross-stitch. They created beautiful bread cloths with specific Christian sayings. They call these "Dorcas Crafts," a reference to Dorcas from the book of Acts. In the Bible, Dorcas was "abounding with deeds of kindness and charity for the widows." Back in the US, Belinda would sell these bread cloths in churches where I would speak. All the money would be used to support these ladies and to provide their families with housing, food, clothing, and school fees.

As the ladies worked on the cross-stitching, Belinda would lead them in Bible studies. She taught them the names of God, and also how to apply these teachings in their children's everyday lives.

First, they talked about *El Roi*, the God who sees all. The omnipresent God who is there. Belinda told them that He was aware of all their circumstances. God saw the persecution they went through. He saw when they had to go to the back of the line whenever there was a shortage of flour, sugar, milk, or water. Why? Because they were refugees from Uganda, living in Kenya.

God saw when no one would hire them. He saw them living in poor conditions, with no electricity. God saw them being rejected. God saw them trying to provide and take care of their children because they did not have an earthly father. Belinda told them that God wanted to be a Father to their children. God is, after all, a Father to the fatherless.

Catherine was one of these women. At her small house, which God had provided, Catherine went home one day and told her young son James what she had learned. Catherine said, "James, you have a Heavenly Father who sees all. He sees what we are going through. He loves you, and wants to be your Father."

Two weeks later, Catherine was heating water to bathe her children. The water was too hot, so she sat the container outside to cool. One of the neighbor's children sat in the hot water, scalding the child. Because Catherine was a refugee, the neighbors said she tried to kill their child.

The "Youth Wingers," a group that took justice into their own hands, came to Catherine's house. One of the men said, "You tried to kill your neighbor's child, so we are going to kill your child."

They grabbed James, and started beating him.

James said, "My Father sees what you are doing, and He does not like it."

The men responded, "You do not have a father. Your father is dead."

James said, "No, my Father sees what you are doing and He does not like it!"

Right at that moment, they stopped beating James.

One of the men explained, "You must have someone looking after you. Because we were coming last night to cut your mother into pieces, but something detained us from coming. We do not do that sort of thing in the daytime. So someone must be looking after you."

They turned around and walked out.

That day, James saw that he did have a Father who sees all. A Father who cares very much for him!

When Belinda first shared this story with me, I was without words. Could I have been as bold as James had been? Could I have looked at my would-be murderers and said, "My Father sees what you are doing."?

If Catherine had not taught her child that he had a Father in Heaven, had she not taught him what she'd learned from Scripture, what might have become of both of them?

That day James was confronted with a threat to his life. He received and believed what he had been taught. Then, when the time came, he acted on the Word of God. James spoke with authority, not his own, but authority based on the teachings he had received. Only the power of God could intervene and speak through a seven-year-old boy to save the lives of two people. The power of *El Roi*.

El Roi. The God who is there. His eyes are not shut. He is aware of all your circumstances. He sees you right where you are.

Do you feel forgotten? That no one sees you? That maybe even God has hidden His face from you? I can assure you that this is not the case. God saw a little boy in Kenya and He sees you too.

How seriously do you hear, receive, believe, and act upon the Word of God? James' life was threatened. But he would not cower under the pressure and fall back upon his own strength. No way!

What will you do?

Will you waiver between doubt and belief, allowing the waves of life to control the way you think, feel, and act? Or will you say with authority, "My Father is watching!"?

30

THIS WALLET WAS LOST, BUT NOW IT'S FOUND

As I have mentioned, I divided the continent of Africa into hubs, or regions. Each region had its own director.

The West Africa regional director was a man named Steve. Steve lived with his family in the nation of Ivory Coast. They lived in Yamoussouko, the administrative capital.

One day Steve was walking on the sidewalk. On that particular road, there was an open pit next to the sidewalk. Such pits were known for having items fall down into them —especially when it rained.

As Steve was walking, he noticed something that looked like a wallet. So he reached down into the open pit and picked up the wallet. He studied it and determined that it was indeed a man's wallet.

Looking inside for some sort of identification, Steve found a large amount of money. He also found a person's name and address, but no phone number. In an effort to reunite the owner with his wallet, Steve returned to his office and wrote the man a letter.

"I have found your wallet. You can come to my office to pick it up." Steve gave the address.

About a week later, a man showed up at his office. He gave Steve his name and said, "I received a letter from you telling me that you had found my wallet." Then, he handed Steve that letter.

"Of course," Steve remembered. He took out the man's wallet and handed it to him.

The man was overwhelmed with joy. He opened the wallet and saw the money. He counted it, discovering it was all still there. He was so excited!

The man explained, "I build furniture. A customer had given me this money as a deposit to build him specific items of furniture. The money was to buy supplies."

Steve wanted to talk further, but the man said he did not have time. He said, "Thank you for finding my wallet and returning it to me! I will come back next week and we'll talk more then."

The man left. Steve was not sure if the furniture builder would come back or not.

But the next week, he did come back. Steve built a relationship with the man. Then, Steve presented the gospel to him, and the man prayed to receive Christ!

Steve met several more times with the furniture builder. He helped him not only to understand the decision he had made, but how to share his faith with someone else. The story does not end there. The man's life was transformed through meeting with Steve.

The man would walk around town, telling the story about his lost wallet. He would pull out his wallet, hold it in the air, and say, "Once this wallet was lost. It was in the open pit, with the other trash beside the road. A man named Steve saw it. He reached down into the open pit and pulled it out. Then, it was found."

The man went on to say to every person he met, "Once this man," pointing toward himself, "was lost. And there was a man named Jesus who reached down into the pit and pulled me up. Once I was lost, but now I am found." Then the man went on to present the gospel.

In what ways has God pulled you out of a pit? What has He rescued you from? Or are you in a pit right now, lost? If you are, God is one prayer away from making you "found."

You can pray right now:

Lord, I have committed sins in my life. I have done things that are wrong. Will you please forgive me for all of my sins? I receive Your Son, Jesus Christ, as my Lord and Savior. I give my life to you. Thank You, Jesus, for saving me!

31

PICK UP YOUR BAG AND COME WITH ME

"Pick up your bag and come with me," the airport security agent said. By his tone, I could tell he meant serious business.

I was in the nation of South Africa, where I had visited our national office in Pretoria. My goal was singular: to bring 1,000 EE lapel pins back to Nairobi. The pins had two question marks on them, and people wore them on their collars or jackets. Since we didn't make the pins in Kenya, I had to fly to South Africa to get them.

The office staff in South Africa had wrapped the pins in the shape of a ball using cellophane tape. It was around the size of a small volleyball. I placed the ball of pins into my carry-on luggage. I had learned that anything put in checked luggage may be removed or stolen.

Upon arriving at the Johannesburg airport to fly back to Nairobi, I checked in at the counter, proceeded to immigration, and then to security. I placed my carry-on baggage on the security belt and moved to the end, waiting to pick up my bag.

As it came out of the X-ray machine, the agent looked at me and said, "Is this your bag?"

I replied, "Yes."

"Pick up your bag and come with me."

I tried to explain. "You probably saw—"

He abruptly interrupted me and repeated his command.

I did as the agent said. I picked up my carry-on bag and walked over to another area, which was located away from everyone else.

The agent, looking quite upset, demanded, "Open your bag!"

I did as instructed, and unzipped my bag to reveal the ball of 1,000 pins wrapped tightly together. And then it hit me—it actually looked like a bomb! *What was I thinking, bringing these on the plane?* I wondered.

"What is this?" he barked.

I took one of the EE pins and showed it to him. I said, "There are many questions in life that people ask. But there are two very important questions. Would you like to know what those two questions are?"

He seemed like he wanted to stay angry with me, but he was also curious. He hesitated before saying, "Yes."

Then I asked him, "Have you come to the place in your life where you know for certain that if you were to die today, you would go to Heaven?"

What was I thinking? If he were to die today! What kind of a question is that to ask when someone thinks you're trying to smuggle a bomb onto a plane!?!

But I was so focused on sharing the gospel that I forgot the seriousness of my situation. The man looked at me and answered, "No."

Then I asked the second question: "If you were to die today and stand before God, and He were to ask you, 'Why should I let you into my Heaven?', what would you say to God?'"

The agent did not have an immediate answer. Finally, he said, "God would not let me into His Heaven!"

I knew the agent needed to get back to work. I had a small EE tract that explained the gospel using those two questions. I gave this small tract to him and said, "You can read this tract. At the end of it, it will ask you if you want to make a decision. If you want to make that decision, it will lead you through a prayer. Then tonight you can have the certainty that someday you will go to Heaven."

I placed the 1,000 metal pins back in my suitcase. As I turned around to look for the agent, he had not gone back to help the next person through security. Instead, he had gone into the break room—I imagine to read the small EE tract.

Our opportunities to share the gospel message may come when we least expect them. We may not even recognize them as opportunities unless we're waiting and watching for a chance to talk about our faith. I know it can be uncomfortable for some, but consider what's at stake —eternity!

Pray for boldness, and pray that God would give you an opportunity to share His message with someone this week. Hopefully, there will be no "bomb scares" involved!

32

THIS MAN WILL RETURN ON THE NEXT FLIGHT TO KHARTOUM

I had invited a man named Peter to fly into Kenya to receive the EE ministry training. Peter was flying in from Khartoum, Sudan, which was his home. We hadn't yet trained anyone from his nation, so I was particularly looking forward to our meeting.

When I arrived at the airport to pick up Peter, I parked in the lot and awaited his arrival. And I waited. And waited. And waited. I knew Peter had made his flight, so I wasn't sure why he wasn't coming out of the airport. I went inside to find out.

When I found Peter, I was even more alarmed than when I thought he was missing. Peter had been detained by an immigration officer.

"He has no Kenyan visa!" the officer said.

I knew that wasn't accurate. I had purchased and sent Peter's airline ticket myself. I had also confirmed that Peter had taken the ticket to the Kenyan embassy in Khartoum to obtain a visa. But I didn't lose my temper.

"I am responsible for Peter," I explained calmly. "He will stay with me, go through my ministry's training, and I will see to it that he is on his departure flight as scheduled."

The immigration officer looked straight at me, and with a cold, hard voice said, "This man will be on the next flight to Khartoum."

The next flight wasn't for another three days, so I had some time. Unfortunately, time was *all* Peter had. He'd have to stay in the airport. Privately, I talked to Peter. I gave him some Kenyan money for food and assured him I'd be back.

I left the airport and drove straight to my office. "Lord," I prayed, "what do You want me to do?"

The thought popped in my mind that if Peter couldn't come to me, I'd go to him. I'd take the training materials to the airport. And we'd get in a little OJT (on-the-job training)! I decided that if it came to that, I'd start with the immigration officer who had denied Peter's entrance into Kenya.

Thinking back now, I could have been arrested for what I did next. But in the moment, it felt right.

I wrote a letter to Kenyan Immigration on my stationary, which stated my name as the director of the ministry for the continent of Africa. I also pressed my rubber stamp on the letter, and signed over the stamp to make it official—the proper procedure in Kenya.

I called several leaders who were helping with our training that week, along with other friends, and I asked them all to pray that I'd be able to present my letter to the immigration authorities. Belinda and I also prayed together.

"I'm not sure what's going to happen," I told her as I left. "To Peter or to me!"

I prayed as I drove to the airport. I prayed as I parked my car. And I prayed before I walked back inside. I had the letter in one hand and my business card in the other. *Only God can change the heart of man!* I thought as I walked back inside and requested to speak with the head of immigration.

Luke 1:37 tells us that nothing is impossible with God. I held that verse in my heart, even as the officer's words rang in my ears: "This man will be on the next flight to Khartoum." I rejoiced despite the challenges ahead, thanking God in advance for what He was about to do.

Miraculously, I was able to meet with the head of immigration himself! Probably because I was wearing a suit, which was not common for passengers in the Nairobi airport. I handed him my card and the letter.

The letter explained why Peter was in Nairobi, what he would do while he was there, what date and time he would return back to the Nairobi airport, and what flight he would return on. What was hard to believe was that I was asking for the authority to receive Peter under my care. Me—a former programmer analyst!

The man requested Peter be brought to him. He asked to see his passport. Without much more thought, he picked up his rubber stamp and approved Peter's visa inside the passport. Then, he directed Peter to go with me and handed me Peter's passport! It all worked out even better than I had imagined!

Peter ended up doing beautifully with the EE training. He learned the gospel presentation and how to implement our ministry in Sudan. Though I didn't get to do OJT with the immigration officer, Peter was able to do OJT in Nairobi. When Peter returned to the airport, he made it through immigration and back home to Sudan with no further problems.

Peter's story reminded me of a trip I took with Belinda when we were in college in 1970. We took a drive from our college town of Athens, Georgia, to Tallulah Gorge. We were there to see Karl Wallenda—a highly-acclaimed, 65-years-young, tight-rope walker—walk from one side of the gorge to the other side. The gorge was almost 1,000 feet deep and a quarter mile wide!

The cable had been put into place and secured on either side. The Great Wallenda, as he was known, stepped onto the cable. As he walked, we all watched, intrigued. We had not come to see him fall. We all expected him to make it safely across, even with the wind blowing.

He walked slowly across to the side we were sitting on, then he walked back across to the other side. He had done it! Just like we knew he would.

If the Great Wallenda had asked me, "Ron, do you think I will make it across the cable?", I would have said, "Yes! I do believe." But if he had said, "If you believe, get on my shoulders and we'll walk across together," I would have said, "No way! Absolutely not!"

When someone says, "I believe in Jesus," is it not the same? I had head knowledge that the Great Wallenda would make it across the cable, but I did not have enough faith to rest the weight of my life on that belief. Similarly, many walk through life with a head knowledge of Christ, but aren't willing to fully surrender their lives to Him, trusting Him with everything.

What about you? Do you operate with a head knowledge of Jesus and who He is? Or do you have total faith and trust in Him? Has there been a complete transfer of trust, from yourself to Jesus, to get you into Heaven? Or do you believe it is by your own good works and deeds that you deserve eternal life?

If Jesus said, "Get on my shoulders," how would you respond? I pray you take some time today to ask yourself that question, and honestly consider your response.

Because His are the only shoulders that can carry us through the gates of Heaven.

33

OFF COURSE

I trained a missionary who then went and trained several other Kenyan pastors.

They decided they would travel by boat on Lake Victoria to one of the islands to share the gospel message with the people there. Lake Victoria borders three nations of Africa: Kenya, Tanzania, and Uganda.

The pastors and the missionary got on a small boat and started across the lake. As they were moving toward the island, a strong wind came, pushing the boat in a different direction. They tried to stay on course, but the wind was too strong, and it looked like a heavy rainstorm was coming.

To get to safety, their boat eventually landed on a random island—not the one they had planned on visiting. They did not realize it at the time, but this island was inhabited.

By now the storm was dumping out gallons and gallons

of rain. They noticed huts on the island where people lived, and ran toward them in hopes of finding shelter. One of the people who lived in one of these huts asked, "What are you doing here?"

"We have come to tell people about God and how they can have eternal life," one answered.

The person who had asked the question said, "I want that!"

Another person in the hut said, "I want that!"

And another person said, "I want that, too!"

The rains stopped. The people came pouring out of the huts. The pastors built a relationship with the islanders and presented the gospel to them. They listened intently. When the pastor asked, "Would you like to receive the gift of eternal life?", many people on the island said, "Yes!"

Many on that island prayed to receive Jesus Christ as their Lord and Savior that day!

When they were finished talking with each other, the missionary and the pastors climbed into the boat and pushed off to return to the mainland.

As the boat began to cross the lake, one of the pastors turned to the others and said, "You know, we thought we were pushed off course, but we were actually pushed onto God's course!"

Could the Lord possibly be asking you, "Are you willing to change the direction you're traveling today to a different course I have prepared for you?"

If you feel like you aren't heading in the direction you wanted to go, invite God to be your navigator. If you put your trust in Him and remain obedient, you can trust that wherever you are, you are exactly where you're supposed to be.

34

WHERE SHOULD I RUN?

If you can recall my opening story from the introduction, I had been held overnight at a layover in Brazzaville, Congo, while I waited for my connecting flight back to Nairobi. It was about 5:30 in the morning, but still dark out. There were no lights in the parking lot. The bench was not very comfortable, but it was better than sitting on the ground.

All was quiet. For a moment.

Then suddenly, I heard the ear-piercing sound of gunfire. I saw a flash of light to my right. It was only about 30 feet away! Then I heard another round of gunfire to my left, followed by more flashes of light.

I prayed, "Lord, where should I run?" I kept thinking, *I should get under the bench.* I listened and heard the answer, "Run into the arms of Jesus, do not move!"

Another shot and a flash of light from the right, then one from the left. I was sitting in between the shots!

I remembered the Scripture, "I will never leave you, nor

forsake you." Also, the words, "Run into the arms of Jesus—
Do not move!" I kept wanting to do something. Get under
the bench. Anything! But no, I remained where I was.

The shooting stopped as quickly as it had begun. It was
then I saw a man to my right, laying on the ground. *He's
dead,* I realized.

Slowly, I got up, picked up my luggage, walked into the
bush, and remained quiet. From the airport entrance,
several people came out, pointing lights toward the bench
and the area. I remained hidden. The people stood around
looking at the man on the ground.

From where I was hiding, I could see the bench and the
surrounding area. I realized, *I was just sitting right between the
two gunmen.*

I remained hidden in the bush for about an hour or so.
During that time I thought, *My initial reaction, my plan when the
shooting began, was to hide under the bench.* But while waiting in
the bush, I saw that if I had climbed under the bench, I
could have been a target for each gunman, who might have
mistaken me for the other person.

When the sun finally crept up the African sky, I came
out of my hiding spot and walked into the airport to fly
back home to Nairobi. I was never so happy to see my
family!

Multiple times I have relived what happened that night.
I could have been injured. I could have been killed.
Someone could have stolen my passport and my
identification.

Belinda, Timothy, and Ann Marie would have never
known what happened to me. Belinda only knew I had gone

to Central African Republic. She never knew I was changing planes in Brazzaville, Congo.

My prayer was, "Lord, where should I run?"

The answer that came to me? "Run into the arms of Jesus—Do not move!"

The arms of Jesus are where I found physical security that night. But they also provide me with spiritual security—hope of eternal life in Heaven.

Where does your security lie? With a job? A spouse? Money? Status?

I pray you're never in the middle of a gunfight in the African Congo, but I do pray you'd seek out the answer to that question with just as much urgency. Your life may not depend on it right now, but your eternal life certainly does.

35

WHY ARE YOU WASTING YOUR TIME ON THAT BEGGAR?

Two days before I was to fly from Nairobi to Kampala, Uganda, our ten year old son Timothy had severe stomach pain.

Belinda and I took him to our doctor to evaluate the situation and determine a plan of action. The doctor thought Timothy may have appendicitis. I asked the doctor, "Are you certain?"

"No," he said. "Let's watch and see."

Belinda and I prayed about whether I should travel to Uganda or not. I was the main leader in the training, and it was our first time being able to go into Uganda. Belinda and I were not certain if Timothy's stomach ache was a spiritual attack or not. After much prayer, we thought I should go.

The training was to be held at a very large church located in Kampala, the capital city. During the training the pastors would learn how to share their faith in Jesus, and how to train their church members to do the same. The pastor hosting the event went on to train several hundred members of his church over the next couple of years.

During the event, a lady who was a member of his church came into our meeting. She asked the pastor, "Can I share what took place over the last two days?"

He asked me, and I agreed it was fine.

The lady was a police officer. Her partner was a police officer too. Together, they would walk the streets of Kampala, making sure everyone was safe.

Two days prior, she was walking with her partner on the streets of Kampala. As they were walking, they came across a beggar, which was quite common. But this situation turned out to be just the opposite!

The beggar asked for help. The lady looked down at the beggar and felt compassion for him. However, her partner looked at her and said, "Why are you wasting your time on this beggar? He can do nothing for you."

She looked at her partner and said, "To God, this beggar's soul is just as important as my soul or yours!"

She stopped and presented the gospel to this beggar. Sitting on the sidewalk on the street of Kampala, the beggar prayed to receive Jesus Christ. The next day the lady police officer returned to the beggar and brought him food and other items he needed.

Once the hand of a beggar, my hand, reached up to God as He reached down to me. He offered me the gift of eternal Life. I received it then, and am eternally grateful.

You may not stand in judgment of a beggar, but what about other people in your life? Do you judge the divorced couple? The young, pregnant girl? The man who lost his job? Their souls are just as precious to God as yours is. It's people like them that God desires us to share His hope with the most—the people who can do nothing for you.

Oh, and Timothy's stomach never hurt again!

36

WHY ARE YOU SO DIFFERENT?

It was about 9:00 A.M. as I sat in the Bulawayo airport waiting for my flight to Johannesburg, South Africa. It was scheduled to depart in two hours, but the plane had not yet arrived.

The passengers for my flight were sitting in a waiting area close to the departure gate. A voice came over the overhead speakers. The announcement was that our flight had been delayed by two hours. There was a chorus of groans as people processed how that delay would impact their schedules.

Half an hour later there was a second announcement—another delay. More groans! The ticket agent said the new departure time would *possibly* be after an additional eight hours. In fact, the airline wasn't even sure if the flight would leave that same evening. In total we were looking at a 10–12 hour delay. Talk about uncertainty and chaos!

When I heard the second announcement, I decided to

remain seated instead of walking to the ticket agent. I was located about twenty-five feet from the counter, and I had a good view of all the action that began to take place!

Immediately, many of the passengers rushed toward the ticket counter. I was glad the agent had a counter to separate him from the out-of-control passengers. When it comes to flying in Africa, and probably in most places around the world, people can become downright mean when things don't go their way. And that's putting it mildly.

The passengers began yelling at the agent and pushing each other to get closest to the counter. It was not a pretty sight! I was sure the ticket agent must be overwhelmed.

What could I do or say?

As I sat, I began thanking God for the situation. I prayed for the agent. And I prayed that the airline might find another plane to create an earlier flight for these enraged people.

I continued to wait. Some passengers left the area. Others were sitting, discussing the situation, and complaining to one another.

After the counter had cleared and the ticket agent was still standing, I decided to walk to the counter and talk. By then the ticket agent was worn out. He saw me approaching and probably thought, *Oh no, not another one!* Well, he was about to be pleasantly surprised.

In talking with him, I sympathized and apologized for the behavior of some of the other passengers. I tried to comfort him, saying, "I know this scheduling change is not your fault. You are doing a good job, trying to give us information. Thank you for your service!"

He seemed shocked and thanked me for understanding.

The hours passed slowly. Eventually, our plane landed and taxied to the gate. Then it was serviced. Once again, the remaining passengers began to check in, but were not yet boarding. While waiting, another passenger came up to me and asked if he could sit down beside me. I agreed.

He said, "I watched the way you spoke to the ticket agent. Why are you so different?"

I considered his words. Then I explained how Jesus helped me handle that and all difficult situations. The passenger seemed interested in listening. I asked, "What do you mean when you say, 'Why are you so different?'"

The passenger said, "I was watching you. You did not race up to the ticket agent and question him. After most of the passengers had left, I saw you go up to him and began talking in a calm manner. You even apologized for the words and actions of some of the other passengers." He repeated his question: "Why are you so different?"

I said, "Each time I heard that the flight was delayed, I prayed and thanked God for this situation."

He said, "I have never heard anyone say you are to thank God for a challenging situation."

I explained that the Bible instructs us to do so. I went on to say, "As I thank Jesus, it releases the power of God into the situation! Then I feel a peace and calmness, knowing that Jesus is handling the problem."

We talked further. The passenger was now open to hearing the gospel. We eventually boarded the flight together, where the passenger received eternal life!

You never know who is watching your actions or hearing your words.

If someone were to watch the way you treat others—people at work, servers in restaurants, other drivers in traffic—what would your actions say about you? Would someone have a reason to say, "Why are you so different?"

Remember that your life is a living testimony of what you believe. Even when no one else is watching, Jesus always is!

37

I WALK WITH YOU—YES?

After several years of being in Africa, we established our children's ministry called "Kids EE." The Kids EE training includes fun activities and teaching lessons designed for children.

In 1996, we held a Kids EE training in Tanzania, a country on the East coast of Africa. Leaders from several area churches were in attendance, along with a large group of children. The training was being led by a woman named Elise, who did a wonderful job with the program.

One day after training, Elise wanted to be alone with the Lord to pray. So she went off by herself and asked, "Lord, I need a touch from you."

Suddenly, Elise felt someone grab her hand. She opened her eyes to see a little boy touching her.

"I walk with you. Yes?" the little boy said.

Elise smiled. "Yes," she answered.

The two walked along, holding hands. But as they were

walking, Elise did not feel a human hand in hers, but the Lord's. He had answered her prayer!

There are times in life when we are not sure what we stand in need of. It is those times that we can ask God to simply be with us—to touch us. God longs to be near to us, He only needs an invitation. Will you ask Him for a touch today?

38

I WANT TO GO HOME

In addition to my duties to EE, I was also involved in other ministries through our local church in Nairobi.

Similar to what I did with EE, I would train members of our church to share the gospel and then take them out for OJT training. We would walk around public areas and share our faith with anyone who wanted to listen. Prior to OJT, we held classes to teach the trainees how to present the gospel. I was the senior teacher of our church's class. Every week I would take two members of the class out for OJT.

One week I was driving to the park to meet my two trainees. Sadly, I was tired. I did not feel like sharing the gospel, and I just wanted to go home. I prayed, "God, please don't let these two trainees be waiting for me. I pray they won't show up so I can just go home."

But wouldn't you know it, when I pulled into the parking lot, there they were—both waiting for me.

I parked my car and approached them. "I need to make

a confession," I said. "I did not want to be here today. I was wanting to go home, but I saw you here and had to stop." I asked for their forgiveness, then I prayed and asked for God's forgiveness too.

One of the trainees spoke up and said, "Ron, I had the same thoughts as you! I did not want to be here today, either. I am also tired and want to go home." We prayed with this man as he asked God's forgiveness for his attitude. Then we got to work!

We walked around the park and came upon a man. After sharing the gospel, we asked him, "Would you like to receive the gift of eternal life?"

"Yes!" he replied.

Together, we led the man in the prayer of salvation. His life was changed forever that day because we did not go home when we wanted to.

I had prayed, "God, I'm really tired, and I want to go home. Please don't let the two trainees be waiting for me."

I am so thankful the Lord said, "No!"

Have you ever prayed and asked God for something that He did not provide? Has it crossed your mind that God knows what's best for you—and what's best for others? God orchestrates our lives to bring Himself glory and make Himself known. The next time you pray and God says, "No," consider that He knows what's best for us and for others, even when we don't!

39

BLIND SINCE BIRTH

During a training in Zimbabwe, many pastors from across the country had gathered to learn how to share their faith and teach their church members to do the same.

As usual, near the end of our training, we took the trainees out for the OTJ portion of our training. For this particular training, we went out into a village. A man named Agrippa was our national director. While in the village, Agrippa and his team came across a woman who was 103 years old. She told them that she had been blind since birth.

Agrippa talked with the lady and asked her if she would like to hear the gospel presentation. She agreed, and Agrippa walked her through the steps. At the end he asked, "Does this make sense to you?"

"Yes," she replied.

"If this is really what you want to do," he said, "then you can pray to God and tell Him what you just told me." Then he asked her to bow her head to pray.

After the prayer, Agrippa opened his eyes to find the lady looking around strangely. "I can see," she said. "I can see!"

Agrippa, unsure of what she meant, said, "Yes! Your spiritual eyes have been opened."

"No!" she replied with enthusiasm. "I can see *you*!"

The lady had received not only salvation, but also her vision! Blind since birth, she could now see! Agrippa was amazed—he had not even prayed for her physical healing!

The woman began walking and leaping. Well, as much as a 103-year-old woman can walk and leap. The people in her village witnessed what happened. Many of them also prayed to receive Jesus as their Savior.

God can still work miracles! And not just in the lives of the young and well, but in the lives of the old and sick. If you stand in need of healing today, regardless of what ails you, God is still the same powerful God He's always been. He can restore you, strengthen you, and heal you. It's never too late for God!

40

WHAT DO YOU WANT ME TO SAY?

I was flying from Nairobi to Harare, the capital city of the nation of Zimbabwe.

After landing in Harare, I walked over to the domestic airport to continue my travel. At Air Zimbabwe's ticket counter, I was standing in line to check in for my next flight. Behind me in the line was a very distinguished gentleman dressed in a suit, probably in his mid-50s.

After I checked in, I walked over to an area with other passengers. I decided to stand before deciding where to sit and wait for the flight.

The distinguished gentleman walked up to me and started a conversation. From talking, I realized he was a very successful businessman, but by no means arrogant. He was a professional.

As we talked further, I discovered that his name was Richard. The last two days he had spoken at a conference of accountants. Richard's specialty was finance and investments.

Several other men in suits came up to him, inviting him to the bar. Richard was not pleased with one of the men and said, "Can you not see I am talking with this gentleman?"

By the way, that was me! A gentleman!

We continued our conversation, and after a while, Air Zimbabwe called our flight number. Time to board! We discovered that we both were on the same flight to Bulawayo. As we boarded the plane, I followed Richard down the aisle. He stopped at his row, as written on his boarding pass. His seat was by the window.

Where was my seat? You probably figured it out. It was next to Richard on the aisle. I knew this was not a coincidence, but as I say, a "God-incident." He put us together!

I did not tell Richard what I specifically did for a living. But I did say, "I am in investments. We invest in people!"

Richard said, "I do the same. I find a person who has accomplished as much as possible in their position. Then I financially invest in them to help the person reach the next level."

At some point, Richard inferred that I was a Christian. After his discovery, the floodgates of Richard's past opened. He shared many of his negative experiences from childhood and his teenage years—some of which took place in a Christian boarding school.

I listened. I listen some more. It was time to redirect the conversation, which I hoped would bring healing to

Richard's life. From Harare to Bulawayo was not a very long flight, so I wondered what I was going to say next.

When I am talking with someone, I remember that the Bible tells me to rejoice always and to pray without ceasing. I was rejoicing in the Lord, because I knew He had brought Richard onto my path. I was also praying—with my eyes open, of course!

I said, "Lord, I know you love Richard with an everlasting love. You created him and desire to touch his life today. I do not know how You plan to do that, but I am open to what You want me to say!" I added, "I know how to present the gospel. But I think You have a specific message for Richard today. What do You want me to say?"

Richard and I talked a couple more minutes. Then specific thoughts came to my mind. The Lord was showing me what to say!

I looked at him and asked, "Richard, do you have a son?"

He responded, "Yes."

I noticed something was off in his answer. "What is your son's name?"

Richard replied, "Robert."

I went on to ask, "Do you mind telling me about your son?"

Richard said that he had not talked to his son for a couple of years. I could tell this saddened him. Richard said he was estranged. I could hear pain in his voice as he answered.

I wanted to be absolutely correct in what I said next, so I was praying diligently to the Lord, "What do you want me to say?" I listened intently. *Here it comes,* I thought. I took a deep breath and let it out.

"Richard, what do your children call you?"

He said, "Dad."

"Richard, wouldn't you love to have Robert say to you, 'Dad, I just want to thank you for all the things you have done for me. I do not want anything from you.' Then Robert would place his arms around you and say, 'Dad, I love you!'"

Tears began rolling down Richard's cheeks—this very successful and wealthy businessman was openly crying on an airplane.

Earlier in our conversation, Richard had told me about his other child—a daughter named Mary. Mary was also alienated from Richard. I knew I had to go to Mary next!

"Richard, earlier you said you have a daughter named Mary. Is that correct? That relationship isn't good either, is it?"

I could tell that was a difficult question for Richard to answer. He said, "Not good."

"Richard, wouldn't you love to have Mary say to you, 'Dad, I just want to thank you for all the things you have done for me. I do not want anything from you.' Then Mary would place her arms around you and say, 'Dad, I love you!'"

By then, Richard was very emotional. I could tell that he was trying to control his feelings by his expression.

I looked directly into his eyes and I said, "Richard, you have a Heavenly Father who is saying to you, 'Richard, I love you. Allow me to place my arms around you. Allow me to heal all those negative memories. Let me hold you tight!'"

I stopped talking. All was quiet except the roar of the jet engines.

Richard was overwhelmed with emotion. I knew he was realizing that He was loved by God in Heaven—that they were not estranged. And that God longed to hug him tightly. I also knew God was working in Richard's heart, healing him and making him whole.

It would only be through reconciling with God that Richard would be able to reconcile with his children. I was confident that God had done a great work on that flight, and that Richard was now ready to contact his children to mend their relationships.

Then together, Richard and I prayed.

The Air Zimbabwe flight turned into its final approach to land in Bulawayo, Zimbabwe. Beside me, Richard was overwhelmed with joy. He had received the touch of the Lord.

I was grateful for the privilege to allow the Lord to speak through me. It was certainly not me coming up with the right words! I had never used those words before in a conversation. Those words were specifically given for Richard that day.

As the plane taxied to our gate, Richard said, "Would you come and stay at my house while you are in Bulawayo? I have never asked anyone to stay."

"Thank you, Richard, I appreciate the invitation. But I am staying with someone else in Bulawayo."

Then Richard asked, "Do you want to use my cellphone

to call anyone?" I thanked him, but explained that someone was meeting me. It was as though he could not do enough for me!

But it was not for me. Actually, it was for Jesus!

What about you? Are you estranged, separated, or alienated from someone you love? Maybe a parent, grandparent, child, or dear friend? It is time to allow Jesus to make reconciliation possible! It all begins with allowing Him to reconcile Himself with you.

Then He will guide you in the next step.

As I looked directly into his eyes, I explained, "Richard, you have a Heavenly Father who is saying to you, 'Richard, I love you. Allow me to place my arms around you. Allow me to heal all those negative memories. Let me hold you tight!'"

Now I say the same to you. Place your name in the blanks:

"_____, you have a Heavenly Father who is saying to you, '_____, I love you. Allow me to place my arms around you. Allow me to heal all those negative memories. Let me hold you tight!'"

And watch as the Lord restores your relationships, beginning with your relationship with Him!

41

LEAVE MY TERRITORY ALONE

We had been introducing EE into the Sub-Saharan nations for several years. But now it was time to introduce our ministry into the countries that were controlled by the religion of Islam. This was a potentially dangerous endeavor.

I had been told about a group of Christian leaders I could contact to make introductions that might get us into the area. It was a dangerous place for Christians to live, so I did not want to put anyone in harm's way. Using the correct channels of communication was very important.

Contact was made on my behalf, and a meeting requested with the North African leaders. Our training was translated into Arabic, and was adapted to be effective in these nations. I was ready to go, but had to wait until it was safe.

Over a period of a year or so, I had been vetted and investigated thoroughly to ensure I would not be a security risk for the North African church leaders. The time had finally come for our introductions! I did not have many details, but I knew I was to fly to Paris, France, then to another city (which I cannot disclose). I booked my flight and was on my way.

I had no idea who would meet me at the airport. I didn't know where I would stay. I had no telephone numbers. They had my flight information and my photo—that was it.

I flew into Paris. Then I flew into another city located along the Mediterranean Sea. Upon landing, someone did meet me at the airport. But I had never met them before. I was trusting God for protection! I was driven to a secure location to meet with the North African leaders.

Over the next few days, we met together, and the meetings went well. During one of our breaks, I was resting in bed. Though I was still, I wasn't asleep.

Suddenly, I heard a voice. "You have done a good job in the Sub-Sahara African nations, but you need to leave my territory alone."

I immediately recognized the voice of Satan. He was trying to convince me not to work in North Africa. Notice how he led with a compliment, trying to persuade me that I had done enough so I wouldn't move forward. Satan is a cunning enemy!

To combat this spiritual attack, I did what the Bible tells us to do: "Resist the devil and he will flee from you. Come close to God and He will come close to you" (James 4:7-9, NASB). It may make you uncomfortable to hear about this experience. But you may also remember that Jesus was actually confronted by the devil. Satan tried to tempt Jesus, but Jesus was faithful to His Heavenly Father. You can read about Jesus' temptation in Matthew 4:1-11 (NASB):

Then Jesus was led up by the Spirit into the wilderness to be tempted by the devil. And after He had fasted for forty days and forty nights, He then became hungry. And the tempter came and said to Him, "If You are the Son of God, command that these stones become bread." But He answered and said, "It is written: 'Man shall not live on bread alone, but on every word that comes out of the mouth of God.'"

Then the devil took Him along into the holy city and had Him stand on the pinnacle of the temple, and he said to Him, "If You are the Son of God, throw Yourself down; for it is written:

'He will give His angels orders concerning You';
   and

'On their hands they will lift You up,
   So that You do not strike Your foot against a stone.'"

Jesus said to him, "On the other hand, it is written: 'You shall not put the Lord your God to the test.'"

Again, the devil took Him along to a very high mountain and showed Him all the kingdoms of the world and their glory; and he said to Him, "All these things I will give You, if You fall down and worship me." Then Jesus said to him, "Go away, Satan! For it is written: 'You shall worship the Lord your God, and serve Him only.'" Then the devil left Him; and behold, angels came and began to serve Him.

Now, back to my story. I left my room and returned to the meetings. I experienced no further issues. I met with different contacts. With their help, we were able to start EE ministries in the North African nations. The enemy had fled and God drew near!

You may never be confronted with an experience like mine. Before moving forward, I'd like to pray for us:

"Dear Heavenly Father, may You bring calmness to any confusion right now. Reveal what is true, and help the reader or listener be open to your Word as recorded in the book of Matthew. Thank You for guiding us. We know we can trust You and receive Your perfect peace, comfort, and understanding. In Jesus' name we pray. Amen."

That day in my room, I was confronted with a challenge. Should I have said to myself, "You know? That voice is right. I should quit now. This is too difficult and risky."? No! I resisted the enemy and drew near to God.

We will all be confronted with obstacles in life when we're tempted to give up. But you can be assured that if you are walking with God, He will provide the means to overcome any challenging circumstance.

If you ever feel as if you are under spiritual attack, read James 4. If you resist the enemy, he must flee. If you draw close to God, it is His good pleasure to draw close to you.

42

I CANNOT STOP TELLING PEOPLE ABOUT JESUS!

We trained several Christians in a particular African nation on how to share their faith. In this nation, the Islamic religion controls everything, including the government. It is against the law to talk to a Muslim about Jesus. If you are reported for such a conversation, you can be arrested and executed.

For security purposes, I will not share the name of this nation.

Several weeks after the training, we received word of something that took place. One of the young men who went through the training later talked to a Muslim about Jesus. The young man was reported to the government. Who reported what the young man had done? It was his own father!

Why would a father report his son's actions to the government? Because his father was a Muslim. As far as this father was concerned, his son was no longer alive. He was considered dead after claiming to be a Christian.

After the report came in, soldiers came to this young man's house. They knocked on the door, asked for his identification, and confirmed his name as reported by his father. The sergeant who was responsible for this group of soldiers told the young man to come outside.

The sergeant read the accusation that was made against the young man, which was true. The young man knew what the punishment was for such an action—execution for talking to a Muslim about Jesus. He knew the seriousness of the situation. But he also knew his responsibility as a Christian to share the story of Jesus.

He was saddened that his own father had reported him to the government. But the young man knew that he must be true to his Savior and Lord, Jesus Christ.

It was time to carry out the punishment. With rope, the soldiers tied the young man's hands behind his back. Then they placed him in a position to receive the punishment.

The soldiers stood some distance away from the young man. They were lined up, as a firing squad would do. The firing squad pointed their guns at him.

The sergeant looked at the young man and said, "If you will deny this Jesus and never speak about Him again, we will consider lessening your punishment." In other words, instead of death, he would be sent to prison.

The young man had a choice: Deny Jesus and never speak about Him again, or confess that Jesus is His Lord and Savior and be executed.

Seriously, as a Christian, what would you do? Would you

stand with the disciples of Jesus? With the many Christians we read about in the early church who were executed, and are now known as martyrs? There are Christians today who are killed regularly for what they believe. Would you stand with them?

The young man stood before the soldiers, all with their rifles pointed at him. He looked over their heads toward the sky, toward the heavens, and prayed silently, "Lord, give me the courage not to deny You!"

Then, with all his strength, with all his might, he cried out, "I cannot stop telling people about Jesus!"

His voice echoed in the distance. Then, silence. For some reason, the sergeant turned to the other soldiers and commanded them to lower their rifles. The soldiers did as commanded. Then, without another word, the sergeant and the soldiers turned and walked away from that young man that day.

Sometime after this happened, we received word that this young man was still telling others about Jesus.

You may never face a firing squad. But you will face situations where you are called to testify of your faith. It may be a simple, subtle situation—at a party, at the office, with a group of friends, at work, or in school. What will you do? By your silence, will you deny Jesus? By your words, will you deny Jesus? By your actions, will you deny Jesus?

The young man prayed silently, "Lord, give me the courage not to deny You!"

Then, with all the strength within him, he said out loud, "I cannot stop telling people about Jesus!"

May we all share in this young man's boldness and courage!

43

CHANGE NAME TO RUTH

We were doing another Kids EE training, this time in Uganda.

Many children were attending the training over the course of several days. There were children from the church hosting us as well as children from other churches in the surrounding area. The children also invited classmates from school, many of whom had never attended a church before.

A young Muslim girl named Zania heard about the Kids EE activities from a friend. During the training, Zania came to understand who Jesus is and what He has done for her. In the training, the children had the opportunity to make the decision of salvation for themselves.

Zania prayed to receive Jesus as her Lord and Savior.

Each afternoon after the training, Zania returned home. Her parents had been Muslims their entire lives. However, they were intrigued by the positive changes in Zania's life.

They noticed gentleness and kindness in the way she cared about her younger brothers and sisters. Zania was different!

After hearing a Bible study about Ruth, Zania said, "I want a name from the Bible. I want to be called Ruth!"

The day before our training was ending, Zania told her parents that she wanted to change her name. They did not immediately agree, but they did listen.

Because of the changes in Zania's life, her parents decided to come with her to the graduation ceremony on the last night. During the ceremony, the pastor shared a clear gospel message. At the end of the message, the pastor said, "If you would like to receive Jesus as your Lord and Savior, come forward!"

You may have guessed what happened next!

Amazingly, Zania's whole family came forward and gave their lives to Jesus. Zania's father looked at her. "You are welcome to change your name to Ruth!" he said.

The pastor then led the name-changing ceremony for several other children. Zania was included. Her new name was Ruth!

All of this happened because Zania's friend invited her to Kids EE.

When was the last time you invited a friend to attend church with you? Participate in a Bible study? Pray together? Sometimes we can view our mission field as people in other cities, states, and countries. But our mission field starts with our immediate surroundings—our friends and family.

Be challenged this week to share your faith with

someone in your life. Like Zania, it could change their entire family!

44

TELL ME MORE ABOUT THOSE TWO QUESTIONS

Every two-and-a-half years in Africa, our family returned to the US for six months.

On our first visit back, I visited the different churches that supported us prayerfully and financially, speaking at many of their services. One of those churches was in Fairfax, Virginia. It was a very large church, and after I spoke, I walked to the back with the senior pastor to say goodbye to the churchgoers as they left.

One lady in her 30s approached me and said, "Tell me more about those two questions you mentioned in your message."

"Certainly," I said. "I am glad to speak with you. Can you meet me in the Fellowship Hall?"

She agreed to wait for me there. After finishing up in the sanctuary, I told Belinda where I was going. I made sure she told the couple driving us from the church to the airport where I was—this was a conversation I didn't need to miss!

I started by building a relationship with the woman. Then, I asked her both questions—if she were certain of her eternal destination and why God should let her into Heaven.

To the latter she replied, "I guess God would let me into Heaven because I am involved in church. I attend Bible study and I am a member here."

After I heard her answer, I said, "I believe that I have important information to help you to make a decision that will change the rest of your life!" Then I presented the gospel.

Outside, the couple was urging Belinda, "If we don't leave now for the airport, you will miss your flight!"

Belinda said, "Ron is presenting the gospel to her. It's very important that he finishes."

The lady said, "Oh, she is already a Christian. She is very active in our church. Ron doesn't need to do all that!"

Belinda remained firm. "Let's let them finish."

When I got to the end of my presentation, I asked, "Does this make sense to you? Would you like to receive the gift of eternal life?"

"Yes!" she responded. Then she prayed the prayer of salvation and received eternal life!

Later, I walked out to Belinda. We got our luggage into the car and the couple drove us to the airport so we could return to Atlanta. Oh, and by the way, we did not miss our flight! We were right on time.

In the Fellowship Hall that day, a lady heard the greatest story ever told about the greatest person who ever lived.

That day, and that day alone, did she receive the gift of eternal life.

Have you made that decision for yourself? Have your friends and family? It is easy to believe that attending church and doing good deeds is enough to get us into Heaven. But the Bible is clear that there is only one way through those narrow gates—through a personal relationship with Jesus Christ.

45

WHAT DO YOU SPECIFICALLY SAY TO A PERSON?

On another trip back to the US in the early 2000s, I was speaking at a breakfast in a major city in Georgia. At the breakfast, there were a number of men from churches of different denominations.

I told several stories that explained how I trained pastors how to share their faith, and how those pastors would then train their church members to do the same. After the meeting ended, several men approached me and thanked me for coming. One gentleman I did not recognize came up to me.

"I'd like to talk to you one-on-one, if that's okay," he said. So we went to sit at an empty table so we could meet privately. Once seated he said, "What do you specifically say to a person when you present the gospel?"

I told him that first I would build a relationship with the person. Then I would ask the person this question: "Have you come to the place in your life where you know for certain that if you were to die today, you would go to Heaven?" I told him I would wait for the person's answer. Then I would ask a second question: "Suppose you were to die today and stand before God and He were to ask you, 'Why should I let you into my Heaven?', what would you say to God?'"

Interestingly, the man answered those two questions out loud. He said, "No, He would certainly not let me into Heaven."

I wasn't asking him to answer, but I was telling him what I would say in leading someone to Christ. I was a bit confused, unsure if he were role-playing or answering seriously. Awkwardly, I said, "Okay. Then I would present the gospel." Sitting there with this man, I shared the gospel like I would in my presentation.

When I got to the end, I said, "Next, I would say to the person hearing me explain the gospel, 'Does this make sense to you?' Then the person would say yes or no."

Well, this man sitting across the table said, "Yes!"

I was asking myself, *Is this man agreeing with me, following along with my story, or is he personally answering the questions for himself?* I still felt uncomfortable, but continued on.

I told him that I would then ask the person, "Would you like to receive the gift of eternal life?"

The man responded with a strong, "Yes!"

"Then I would go through the clarification to make sure the person understood the decision the person was making," I said. I went through the clarification with him. Still feeling uncomfortable, I said, "Next, I would say to the person, 'I can lead you in prayer and you can tell God what you just told me.' Is this what you want to do?"

I was sitting there thinking, *What will he say next?* Amazingly, the man said, "Yes! I would like to receive the gift of eternal life right now!"

There I was in a major city in Georgia, talking to a group of men I assumed to be believers. Then privately, one-on-one, a man heard the gospel and prayed to receive the gift of eternal life!

After praying, the man thanked me and left.

Before I left the men's breakfast, I asked the senior pastor of the church where the meeting was held if he knew the man.

"Oh yes," he said. "He is the Chairman of the Board of Directors at a bank, and he is an active member of my church."

The Chairman of the Board of Directors wanted to hear *specifically* what I said when I led others to Christ. But more importantly, he wanted to know for himself so that he could make a decision.

At different times, people will come across your path. It may be on an airplane, which happens to me quite frequently. It may be on a golf course. It may be at a ballgame where your children or grandchildren are playing. It may even be in your home when a service person has come to do a specific task. It could be at a swimming pool. Maybe it's someone in your neighborhood who needs to hear the gospel.

Are you prepared to lead someone to the gift of eternal life? Right now, take a few minutes, and write out specifically what you would say to a person who asked you what you believe and why. Then you'll be prepared the next time someone needs an answer!

46

CAN YOU INTERPRET MY DREAM?

I traveled to Malaysia to meet with several of our leaders. There aren't many Christians in Malaysia. Islam is the majority religion, and also the official religion of the country.

A young man met me at the airport and drove me to my hotel. We talked about different events which had happened in our lives.

Normally, I do not ask this specific question, but this time I did. I asked, "How did you become a Christian?"

He said, "Growing up, everyone in my family was Muslim. At age 18, I thought everyone should have a religion."

When he made that statement, I thought, *That is a strange belief, especially for an 18-year-old.* I did not mention what I was thinking, but listened to his story.

He continued. "One night I had a dream. Someone came to me in my dream and said, 'You do not need a religion, you need a relationship!' The next day I thought, *Who can I share this dream with that might be able to interpret it?* For some reason a Christian friend came to my mind. I called and asked if we could meet. He agreed.

"Before telling the dream to my Christian friend, I said, 'I think everyone should have a religion!'"

Then he told his friend about his dream.

The young man paused in telling his story and said to me. "Ron, earlier in our conversation I mentioned to you that I thought everyone should have a religion!"

I said, "Yes, very interesting! Please continue your story."

The young man said to his Christian friend, "Last night I had a dream. Someone came to me in my dream and said, 'You do not need a religion, you need a relationship!'"

He said, "I asked my Christian friend, 'Can you interpret my dream?' After hearing the dream, my friend prayed, asking for the interpretation and what to do next. My Christian friend prayed this prayer out loud. I could hear what he was asking of his God.

"My Christian friend said to me, 'In your dream, Jesus was the One who was talking to you. He said to you, "You do not need a religion, you need a relationship."'"

"Then my Christian friend shared with me how to have a relationship as he shared the gospel."

The young man said, "I prayed to receive a relationship with Jesus. I accepted Jesus as my Savior and Lord."

God had used a dream and its interpretation to bring this young man into a relationship with Him. It was a very interesting car ride for sure!

Just like that 18-year-old, people are waiting to hear a word from God. You may not realize it, but this is true for the people around you. The person may be your neighbor, a family member, or a co-worker. The person could be someone you bump into today at the library or in the carpool line.

Are you ready to help this person? Have you nurtured your own relationship with Jesus? Have you prepared your mind and heart to share about your *relationship* and not your *religion*?

Maybe you don't feel worthy or adequate to share the gospel. In the Old Testament God told Moses to go to Pharaoh. Moses questioned his own ability. Moses said, "Who am I, that I should go to Pharaoh?" Moses did not feel confident in himself.

Moses questioned if the sons of Israel would receive him. "What if they ask my name?" Moses worried. "What if they ask who I am?"

"Tell them the I AM has sent you," God told him.

Do you know what the word *impossible* breaks down into? "I'm" ("I" "Am") "Possible". You may not feel like you have what it takes to share your faith with others, but the great "I AM" does! He can work through you. When you depend fully on God, nothing is impossible!

47

REACHED DOWN AND PULLED ME UP

In 2010 Belinda and I were blessed to be able to take a trip alone, just the two of us. This was a very rare, very special occasion. I was looking forward to spending quality time with my wife!

We had several days booked in Australia at the Hyman Island Resort. The island and the resort were beautiful. The food was delicious and we were having an incredible time together. We were both very grateful.

One day on the beach, we noticed a family of four playing together—a mom, dad, son, and daughter. The husband walked up to us and began a conversation. He told us his name was Bill.

While talking with us Bill said, "I plan to rent a small catamaran and take my children out to sea. Would you like to join me?" Belinda and I had already noticed a couple of small catamarans in the water that people were sailing.

I said to Bill, "I have never sailed a catamaran, have you?"

Bill said, "No. But I think we can do it!"

Neither of us had ever sailed a catamaran, but Bill seemed confident enough for the both of us! We rented the small catamaran for an hour. The ones that we could see all stayed close to the shore. We decided to do the same.

As I mentioned, it was small in size. Only four of us fit. Bill took the lead. Belinda and Jane, Bill's wife, remained on the shore and chatted while we sailed. Though, of course, Belinda kept an eye on us at all times!

Bill seemed to pick up how to sail the small catamaran. We were tacking back and forth, parallel to the shoreline. The children were laughing as Bill and I continued to move from one side to the other, depending on the sail and the wind.

Then, without warning, the sail flipped to the other direction, knocking Bill and me off into the water. Bill and I grabbed ropes in the water to keep connected to the catamaran. The laughter had stopped. As I was being dragged behind the boat, I could see fear in the eyes of the children.

On shore, Belinda and Jane saw what was happening. They ran over to the person who rented us the catamaran. Belinda said, "I think they are having problems!" She pointed to our catamaran.

Bill, who was quite strong and about twenty years younger than I was, worked his way up the rope to pull himself out of the water. He immediately took control of the sail and sat down, exhausted.

By then I had made it to the side of the catamaran. I was worn out. I tried to pull myself up out of the water, but I couldn't.

Bill needed to keep tacking with the sail to keep us from traveling further out to sea. He turned to me. "Can you pull yourself up?"

I tried again, but had no strength left. I could tell that without some help, I wouldn't survive.

"Can you help me?" I asked. "I can't pull up!"

Without losing control of the sail, Bill turned his attention to me. Bill reached down, grasped my right arm, and pulled me up out of the water to safety. He literally saved my life!

Belinda and Jane, watching from the shore, sighed in relief.

I regained my strength on the catamaran, and we continued to sail. We ended up staying out the entire hour and enjoying the remainder of our time together. And though we were laughing with the children again, I knew what had almost taken place.

We returned the catamaran and decided to meet Bill and Jane for dinner. We talked about all sorts of topics, including Christianity, then I retold the story from the catamaran.

When I got to the part where I realized I would drown without help, I said, "Bill reaches down into the water, grabs my arm, and literally pulls me to safety." Then I looked at Bill and said, "Thank you!"

Bill was kind, and he made light of what he had done.

But what had happened that day was real—it was lifesaving. My life!

I looked at Bill and Jane and simply said, "What happened today reminds me of a man named Jesus, who years ago reached down and pulled me up to safety. At that time, I truly became a Christian."

We talked further and enjoyed the rest of the evening together with our newfound friends.

Maybe someone from the shore could have sailed another catamaran out and eventually reached us. Maybe . . . maybe not. What I do know for a fact is that when I was being dragged by the catamaran in the swift and strong Indian Ocean, a man named Bill reached down into the water, grabbed my arm, and pulled me to safety.

What I also know for a fact is that Jesus has done something even more important. He has pulled me up from drowning in sin and into safety for this life, and for eternity! May I always tell the story of Jesus' rescue!

No, I did not lead Bill and Jane in the prayer for salvation that night. But that is not always God's plan. Sometimes He wants us to plant a seed.

I'll do this at restaurants all the time. I will tell the server, "We are Christians and we are about to pray and thank God for our meal. Is there anything you would like us to pray for you?" I do this in a calm voice. Time after time, the server will ask us to pray for something specific. If not then, at some other time in the meal.

By the way, if you are going to tell someone in the service industry that you are a Christian, please leave a large tip. It makes a difference!

Bill reached down, grabbed my arm, and pulled me up to safety.

A man named Jesus also reached down and pulled me up to safety for this life and for eternity.

Both stories are exciting to share. But it is my prayer that in sharing them, a seed is always planted.

Are you prepared to plant a seed today?

48

YOU WANT ME TO DO WHAT!?!

The pastor of a church said to me, "Ron, I want you to bless this weed eater at the worship service."

My first thought was, *You want me to do what!?!*

Let me back up a bit. It was 2013, a few years since I'd been promoted to Senior Vice President of EE. My job now was to work closely with the vice presidents of each continent—the men and women who were doing my previous job!

I was at EE's training center in Fiji, which is an island in the Indian Ocean. For the last two weeks, we had been training our national directors from nations all over the world.

Several of us were going to different locations to preach that Sunday morning. I was going to a small island. The driver took me to where the land ended at a river. I got out of the car and transferred to a river taxi. It was actually just a small boat with an outboard motor on the back. I sat in the front—the only passenger.

We traveled through several small rivers to reach my destination. When I arrived, the pastor met me. We walked to his small house located next to the church. The house was built on top of posts, which allowed for any flooding that might take place. The people were already singing in the small church. But instead of going into the service, the pastor led me up the stairs and into his house.

We went inside and talked for several minutes. Then, the pastor stood and walked over to pick up what we in America call a weed eater. In Australia, they call it a "whipper snipper," which I actually prefer!

"Ron, I want you to bless this weed eater at the worship service."

I had no context for the man's request, but I knew he was serious. So I needed to take it seriously.

Before the service, the pastor placed the weed eater on the platform. He lifted it up so everyone in the church could see. Then he placed it back on the platform and turned to me. Everyone was watching . . . waiting for me to bless the whipper snipper.

"Lord," I prayed, "what do You want me to say?"

As I rose, I believe the Lord gave me these words: "Heavenly Father, may this weed eater be used to cut a path from the surrounding villages to the church so that many people will be able to come and hear the gospel."

Next, the congregation sang a song, then I gave the message with a gospel presentation.

In the front two rows on the right side were seated

several young men. At the very back of the church, I saw an older gentleman not seated, but standing against the wall.

When I gave the invitation for people to ask Jesus to come into their life as Savior, the man who was standing by the back wall of the church came forward. So did the eight young men who were sitting in the front two rows. The congregation began singing, clapping, and praising God for what was happening that morning. Truly, it was a celebration of nine people who came to receive Jesus Christ.

When the service was over, I walked back out to the river taxi. I waved goodbye to the congregation, who were standing on the banks of the river. It was a special time!

Traveling through the different narrow rivers, I eventually arrived back at the location where I had entered the river taxi earlier that morning. The driver and I both got out of the boat and stepped onto the dry land. The driver told me to remain there while he contacted someone to pick me up and return me to the training center.

As I was waiting, a young man walked up to me. I'm not sure where he came from. He was not in a car, but had walked there. No one else was around. He asked, "Are you a preacher?"

I thought, *Okay, but what does he want from me?*

I answered him, "Yes."

He then asked, "How do I become a Christian?"

In asking him a few questions, I realized, the young man was serious. I presented the gospel to him and he prayed to receive Jesus.

Literally, the timing was perfect. As soon as the young man finished praying, a car arrived.

What perfect timing! What a perfect day! What a perfect, beautiful morning and afternoon I had the opportunity to experience!

I remind myself that *this* was not just another day, but a gift. It was a special day filled with God's faithfulness. But what day isn't?

As we walk through each day, God wants us to view our time on earth as an opportunity—a gift. He doesn't want us to just "get by," but to thrive! He wants to use us in His plan to reach as many for Christ as will listen.

What has your day been like today? Do you view it as "just another day," or as a gift that you can live out for your Father in Heaven?

49

DO YOU THINK GOD HAS A PURPOSE FOR MY LIFE?

While back in the US, I wanted to have our slow dial-up internet upgraded. I called Comcast and asked them to install high-speed internet so I could use it in my office at home.

The technician arrived and looked around. Based on what he saw, he assumed correctly that I am a Christian. After the installation he said, "When I meet religious people, I like to ask them a question."

I thought, *Oh no, he is going to ask me a difficult question that I will not be able to answer.*

But I politely said, "Okay, what is your question?"

He surprised me by saying, "Do you think God has a purpose for my life?"

I was caught off guard, but able to answer immediately. "Yes, I do believe God has a purpose for your life." Then I said, "Before we discuss that purpose, may I ask you a question?"

He agreed, "Yes."

I led him through the gospel presentation. "You look like you are in very good health," I said. This man was well over six feet tall, very muscular, and in his late 20s or early 30s. I continued, "You will probably live quite a long time, but if you were to die today, what reason would God have to allow you into His Heaven?"

He pulled up the sleeve of his shirt and showed me a mark there. He said, "I was in downtown Atlanta in a crowd of people. Someone with a gun started shooting. This mark is from a bullet that hit my arm."

He had faced a possible death! *Appropriate question, then,* I thought.

Then he said, "No, I do not know for certain. Actually, I know that I would not go to Heaven."

I went on to say, "May I share with you how I came to know for certain that I will go to Heaven, and how you can know that too?"

His response was, "Yes."

I led him through the remaining steps before looking at him and saying, "If it is okay with you, let us kneel down together next to that chair."

He agreed.

We knelt down by the chair. I prayed for him, then I led him in a salvation prayer. He repeated after me. Then at the end, I closed out the prayer.

I looked at him as we stood up. "Welcome to the family of God."

We chatted a bit more before he thanked me. I thought he was ready to leave, but he was not finished.

He said, "Can I ask you another question?"

I said, "Yes."

He said, "I am living with a lady, and we are not married." He went on to say, "She gave birth to my two children."

I knew what was coming next!

"What should I do?" he asked.

I said, "You have just become a Christian. You just talked to God in your prayer. Why don't we kneel down again and *you* ask God what He wants you to do?"

He agreed. We knelt down next to the chair. Then he prayed, asking God to tell him what he should do. He finished his prayer and we both stood up.

I said, "What did God tell you?"

"God said I should marry her!" he replied. He agreed with God's advice. His first official prayer as a Christian!

We talked a few more minutes. Then the Comcast technician left my house. I had received high-speed internet, but what the man had received was far more valuable!

Are you ready to be the catalyst, the vessel, the person who will allow the Lord to be His representative? Do you recognize that you are an ambassador for Christ? The one who speaks on His behalf?

Recognize today the importance of your role! Be ready to be used by the God who makes us worthy of that calling.

50

DO YOU HAVE A CAR FOR SALE?

We were back in the United States and I was having problems with my car. It was an older Mitsubishi that I had owned for several years.

I took it to the owner of a local auto shop. His mechanic had worked on our vehicles a good bit over the years. The owner was an honest man, who we trusted completely. He was also a Christian and his pricing was fair. Actually, he was better than fair to us, knowing that we were missionaries. He actually supported us financially in our mission work as well.

I explained the car's problem. After sitting at a stop sign or a traffic light, I would press the gas pedal and nothing would happen. The car did not immediately move forward. This did not always happen, but it was happening more and more frequently. Whenever this happened, I would continue to push the gas pedal, and eventually the car would move forward.

This situation was unsafe, and actually quite dangerous. I left the car there so the owner and the mechanic could determine what needed to be done. Then I received the dreaded call—it would cost more to fix the car than the car was worth.

After discussing it further, I asked the owner of the shop what I should do. I couldn't sell the car, knowing of its condition. The owner graciously offered to buy it from me, likely for its working parts.

Belinda and I have always believed that God would provide for our needs, and this was no different. I thanked God for the situation and for how He would surely provide.

I prayed, "Lord, thank You that You are working out a plan. I do not know what that plan is. You know my needs. I do not know how You are going to solve this situation, but I know You will. I rejoice in You. You are in control."

A week later, I was praying about several matters. One matter, of course, was a car for me. I felt the Lord say, "Call your close friend Ron and ask him if he has a car for sale."

I thought, *Ron is not a car mechanic. He is not a used car salesman. He is not a new car salesman.*

Ron was retired. He was a former partner in an international professional services firm. He had nothing to do with the automobile industry.

But I have learned to obey the Lord no matter how absurd His still, small voice may sound. I called my good friend Ron. I asked about him and about his wife. Then I said, "Ron, this question may be strange, but do you have a car for sale?"

Then I waited for his answer. There was silence on his

end. It seemed to last forever, but it was really not very long. Still, he did pause before answering, which gave me a little time to sweat.

"Well," Ron said, "actually, I do!"

Then Ron told me the story of his car for sale. "The car is in excellent condition, only a couple of years old, with very low mileage—under 20,000."

I asked why he planned to sell it. Recently, someone had hit his car in the back. The car had been repaired and repainted. Good, but still a problem for Ron. His wife was extremely sensitive to different odors. Though Ron couldn't tell a difference, his wife was unable to ride in the car due to the smell of the paint.

So he needed to sell the car—a red, two-door Toyota Solara. Almost like a sports car.

Can you imagine a missionary driving up in a red sports car to a church that gives financial support for his family and ministry? Have you ever heard the saying, "Lord, You keep him humble, and we will keep him poor?"

Actually, that is not a very nice statement. I am not aware of any of our personal supporters ever saying that about us—it is kind of a funny saying though!

Ron was also one of our generous financial supporters. He and I talked further. He decided to sell me the car at a much, much lower price than its value.

Later, as I was driving this red sports car, the conversations it started with my passengers were interesting. Some would say, "I would never expect you to be driving a red-colored car!" They never even mentioned the type of car. It was the color, they said, that did not seem to be me.

The car has become an opportunity to give a testimony of God's faithfulness regarding how He supplied our need. I tell the story quite frequently—even to our 18-year-old grandson and our 14-year-old granddaughter! I never want to miss the opportunity to give God praise for what He has done.

What about you? Are you quick to give God credit for all He has done for you and all He has given to you? Do you think it's because of your hard work that you have anything at all? We know from Scripture that isn't the case—all we have is owned by God. It's on lease to us through His goodwill.

What is something you could use as a testimony to God's faithfulness?

EPILOGUE

A JOURNEY OF GOD'S FAITHFULNESS

Remember my prayer in July 1975?

"I will be anything You want me to be. I will go anywhere You want me to go. I will do anything You want me to do."

Then the Lord said to me, "I will use you to reach hundreds of thousands of people for Me!"

Thirteen years of preparation followed, which you have read about in several stories in this book. Then in August of 1988, our family of four moved to Nairobi.

What happened in Africa? We saw the accomplishments of God, which far exceeded our expectations!

Dr. D. James Kennedy, the founder and president of the EE International ministry, wanted to be active in all 53 African nations (actually, in all the nations of the world).

Goal accomplished! In December of 1995, two of my leaders crossed the border and drove to Tripoli, Libya. They trained two people who started the EE ministry there. Libya was the last, bringing the total to 53—we had made it into all 53 nations in Africa.

But it did not stop there!

From August of 1988 when our family moved to Africa, until I closed this chapter of our lives with the Evangelism Explosion ministry in January 2017, the following was accomplished in Africa:

- 4,338 training events for pastors, youth, and children
- 264,621 church leaders trained at these events
- An estimated 24.5 million people prayed to receive Jesus as Savior in local churches

By 1996, Evangelism Explosion had accomplished its goal of planting the gospel in all 211 nations of the world.

They continue their great work of evangelism throughout the world, and we continue to say, "To God be the glory for what He has done!"

A PERSONAL EXHORTATION

WORDS OF ENCOURAGEMENT AND CHALLENGE TO THE
READER

I pray the stories in this book have drawn you closer to the Lord, as you walk daily with Him, the author and perfecter of our faith.

May you not only embrace the Gospel and know that Jesus loves you with an everlasting love. May you be propelled forward to apply the precepts learned into your everyday life.

May you walk with and experience the intimacy with God, as He leads you into adventures that bring joy, strength, encouragement, fulfillment and perfect peace.

May you be ready to present Jesus to others as they see your deeds and hear your words anytime, anywhere, in season and out of season, no matter what the situation.

If I may call you, my friend, may you be encouraged to walk in Jesus' steps, "A Way of Life" that goes "On and On" through you from generation to generation.

My friend, you may ask, "You Want Me to Do What!?!" Be ready to say confidently, "Yes! I am ready!" Why? "Because I know You, Lord, will be with me, and I can and will trust You!"

My friend, may your new adventure begin...

A BRIEF GOSPEL PRESENTATION

You may be asking, "Ron, What is the Gospel? What did you say to the different people in your stories?" Each person I talked to is different, so no two conversations were exactly the same.

However, what follows are the five core points, along with the appropriate Scriptures I shared after building a relationship with the individual.

1. Heaven is a free gift. It is not earned or deserved.

The Scriptures say, "…The free gift of God is eternal life in Jesus Christ our Lord." (Romans 6:23 NASB)

"For by grace you have been saved through faith, and that not of yourselves, it is the gift of God, not as a result of works that no one can boast." (Ephesians 2:8-9 NASB)

2. All are sinners and cannot save themselves.

"For all have sinned and fall short of the glory of God." (Romans 3:23 NASB)

"Therefore you are to be perfect, as your heavenly Father is perfect." (Matthew 5:48 NASB)

I don't know about you, but I am definitely not perfect.

3. God is merciful and does not want to punish us. God is also just, therefore must punish sin.

"I have loved you with an everlasting love." (Jeremiah 31:3 NASB)

"God (I) will by no means leave the guilty unpunished." (Exodus 34:7 NASB)

It seems we have a problem. On one hand God loves us, but on the other hand God must punish sin. God solved this problem in the Person of Jesus Christ.

4. Who is Jesus? Jesus Christ is the infinite God-Man. Jesus is both God and Man.
What did Jesus do? He died on the cross to pay

the penalty for our sin and rose from the grave to purchase a place for us in Heaven.

"In the beginning was the Word (Jesus), and the Word was with God, and the Word was God... and the Word became flesh, and dwelt among us...." (John 1:1,14 NASB)

"All of us like sheep have gone astray, each of us has turned to his own way. But the Lord has laid on Him (Jesus) the iniquity (sin) of us all." (Isaiah 53:6 NASB)

Now He offers us eternal life as a free gift.

How do we receive that gift?

5. By Faith, Saving Faith.

Saving Faith is not head knowledge. It's not merely intellectual assent to a number of historical facts.

Head knowledge is good but is not Saving Faith. Saving Faith is not temporal faith, trusting God for temporary situations, such as travel, family, physical needs. This is good but it is not Saving Faith.

Saving Faith is trusting in Jesus Christ alone. Trusting in what He has done to get us into Heaven.

"...Believe (trust) in the Lord Jesus, and you shall be saved. ..." (Acts 16:31 NASB)

Transfer your trust from what you have been doing to what Jesus has done for you.

WHAT ABOUT YOU?

These are the five core points I shared.

Hopefully, this has been helpful to understand the Gospel. For some of you, it will give you information to share with someone else.

For some it may give you a clear understanding to make your decision. Like those in the stories, you may be ready to answer the question I asked people many times, "Would you like to receive the gift of eternal life?" If this is what you want to do, you can pray this prayer:

Heavenly Father, thank you for offering me the gift of eternal life. I know that I am a sinner, and I cannot save myself. I believe that Jesus died on the cross and paid the penalty for my sin. I now transfer my trust from what I have been trusting in, to trusting in Jesus alone for what He has done for me. I now repent of (turn from) my sin and receive the gift of eternal life. In Jesus name I pray. Amen.

If this was your decision and prayer, please tell someone you know who is a Christian. It will be a great encouragement to that person. It will also begin to strengthen your faith in Jesus as you begin this walk. As I said in one of my stories, "Where should I run? Run into the arms of Jesus!"

MORE INFORMATION AVAILABLE:

If you want to know more about the Evangelism Explosion training, and the complete EE Gospel Presentation which I taught, used for so many years, and continue to use in my daily walk, you will find much more information at, www.evangelismexplosion.org

RECENT RELEASES FROM CALLED WRITERS

CALLED WRITERS
CHRISTIAN PUBLISHING

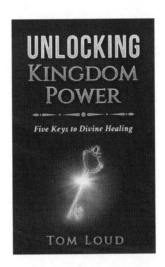

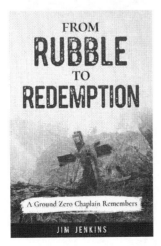

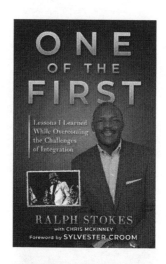

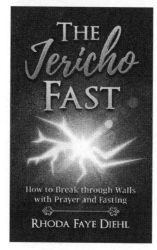

NOTES

3. Please Send Rain, Lord

1. https://en.wikipedia.org/wiki/Szas56kmtate_of_Georgia_Building

20. Do Not Come

1. Lemmel, Howarth Helen. "Turn Your Eyes upon Jesus." (*The Humnal 1982*, Church Hymnal, 1985. *Hymnary.org*, https://hymnary.org/text/o_soul_are_you_weary_and_troubled

ABOUT THE AUTHOR

Ron Tyler and his family were missionaries to the continent of Africa for many years. Ron served as the Vice President of Africa for Evangelism Explosion International, where he was responsible for spreading the gospel over the entire continent. In that role, Ron pioneered a new, simple, and direct method of evangelism that resulted in millions of souls saved.

After Ron served ten years as a United Methodist pastor in the USA, his wife, Belinda, and their two children, Timothy and Ann Marie, moved to Nairobi, Kenya, where they served as missionaries for the ministry of Evangelism

Explosion International. Under Ron's leadership, the ministry was started in 48 nations in Africa. While introducing this ministry, Ron also created a team to further develop and oversee all 53 nations of Africa.

After eight years, Ron and his family returned to the US, and he continued as the Vice President. Later Ron became the Senior VP, responsible for the leadership of the ministry worldwide.

During Ron's time with EE International, he wrote and created materials and training to further develop the ministry's leadership throughout the world. During his leadership in Africa, he created, wrote, and taught the FlipChart training for illiterates and semi-literates. This training helped one to share their faith in Jesus Christ without being able to read or write. The material has been translated in multiple languages throughout Africa and in other parts of the world.

The last five years of Ron's time with EE International, he created, developed, and taught Coaching Training materials for all staff worldwide. The materials have been translated in Spanish, French, Portuguese, Russian, Hindi, Indonesian, Swahili, and multiple other languages. In Ron's lifetime he has spoken multiple times in 56 nations on six continents to Christian leaders from 144 nations.

Ron holds a Master of Divinity Degree (cum laude) and a Doctor of Ministry Degree, both from Emory University.

Ron and Belinda live in the Atlanta area. Timothy, their son, passed from earth to Heaven in 2018. Ann Marie, their daughter is married to Casey, who have given them three wonderful grandchildren: Fisher, Macy, and Finley.

Made in the USA
Columbia, SC
19 February 2023

12696551R00162